Sunday Missal for Young Catholics 2012

I want to know Jesus better.

This missal will help you take part in the Mass on Sundays and important feast days. Pages 2 to 32 contain the words and explain the gestures that are the same for every Mass. The rest of the book gives you the readings and prayers for each Sunday of the year.

Look over the readings with your family before you go to church. This is an excellent way to use this book and a wonderful way to prepare for Mass.

The most important thing about this little book is that it will help you to *know Jesus better*. Jesus came to bring God's love into the world. And his Spirit continues to fill us with love for one another.

We hope the short notes in this book will help you to participate more fully in the Mass. May the Mass become an important part of your life as you grow up, and may the readings and prayers you find in this missal inspire you to love and serve others just as Jesus did.

What we need to celebrate the Mass

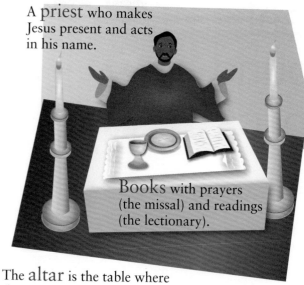

A **priest** who makes Jesus present and acts in his name.

Books with prayers (the missal) and readings (the lectionary).

A group of Christians. You are a Christian by your baptism.

The **altar** is the table where the priest consecrates bread and wine.

The **ambo** is the place where the Word of God is proclaimed.

Two **cruets**, or small containers, one full of water and the other full of wine.

Holy vessels

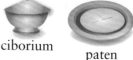

chalice

ciborium

paten

Bread and wine

The Mass is the commemoration of what Jesus did during the Last Supper with his disciples, before he died. The bread is shaped like a small disk and is called a "host."

The four main parts of the Mass

On the following pages you will find the words that the priest says and the responses we say together during each part of the Mass. You will also find explanations and responses to many questions that people ask about the Mass.

Gathering Prayers

The Lord brings us together.
We ask God for forgiveness.
We give glory to God.

The Word

We listen to the Word of God.
We profess our faith.
We pray for the whole world.

The Eucharist

We offer bread and wine to God.
We give thanks to God.
We say the Lord's Prayer.
We share the peace of Christ.
We receive Jesus in communion.

Sending Forth

The Lord sends us home to live the Gospel.

The Lord brings us together

We come together in church with family, friends, neighbours, and strangers. We are here because Jesus has invited us to be here.

When the priest comes in, we stand and sing. Then we make the sign of the cross along with the priest.

Priest: In the name of the Father, and of the Son, and of the Holy Spirit.

Everyone: Amen.

Sometimes, the words can change a bit, but usually the priest will say:

Priest: The grace of our Lord Jesus Christ, and the love of God, and the communion of the Holy Spirit be with you all.

Everyone: And with your spirit.

Why do we celebrate Mass on Sunday?

Jesus rose from the dead on Sunday, the day after the Sabbath. This is why Christians gather on that day. Over time, people started to call it "the Lord's day."

Why do we celebrate Mass in a church?

Churches are built specially for Christians to gather in. If needed, Mass can be celebrated in other places: a home, a school, a plaza, a jail, a hospital, a park…

Why do we need a priest to celebrate Mass?

We believe that Jesus is present in the person of the priest when Christians gather for the Mass. He presides over the celebration of the Lord's supper in the name of Jesus Christ.

Standing

We stand to welcome Jesus who is present among us when we gather in his name.

The sign of the cross

With our right hand we make the sign of the cross (from our forehead to our chest, from our left shoulder to our right) and say "In the name of the  Father, and of the Son, and of the Holy Spirit." This is how all Catholic prayer begins.

Singing

This is a joyful way to pray together.

We ask God for forgiveness

We speak to God and we recognize that we have done wrong. We ask forgiveness for our misdeeds. God, who knows and loves us, forgives us.

Priest: Brothers and sisters, let us acknowledge our sins, and so prepare ourselves to celebrate the sacred mysteries.

We silently recognize our faults and allow God's loving forgiveness to touch us.

Everyone: I confess to almighty God, and to you, my brothers and sisters, that I have greatly sinned, in my thoughts and in my words, in what I have done and in what I have failed to do, *(tap the heart)* through my fault, through my fault, through my most grievous fault; therefore I ask blessed Mary ever-Virgin, all the Angels and Saints, and you, my brothers and sisters, to pray for me to the Lord our God.

Priest: May almighty God have mercy on us, forgive us our sins, and bring us to everlasting life.

Everyone: Amen.

Priest: Lord, have mercy.

Everyone: Lord, have mercy.

Priest: Christ, have mercy.

Everyone: Christ, have mercy.

Priest: Lord, have mercy.

Everyone: Lord, have mercy.

Confess

We recognize before others that we have turned away from God, who is love.

Mercy

We know God is full of mercy — that he loves us even when we have sinned. God's mercy is always there for us.

Amen

This is a Hebrew word meaning "Yes, I agree. I commit myself."

Lord

This is a name that we give to God. Christians call Jesus "Lord" because we believe he is the Son of God.

Christ or Messiah

In the Bible, these words designate someone who has been blessed with perfumed oil. This blessing is a sign that God has given a mission to the person. Christians give this name to Jesus.

Tapping our heart

This is a way of showing we are very sorry for our sins.

7

We give glory to God

We recognize God's greatness when we say "Glory to God." This prayer begins with the hymn the angels sang when they announced Jesus' birth to the shepherds.

Everyone: Glory to God in the highest,
and on earth peace to people of good will.

We praise you,
we bless you,
we adore you,
we glorify you,
we give you thanks for your great glory,
Lord God, heavenly King,
O God, almighty Father.

Lord Jesus Christ, Only Begotten Son,
Lord God, Lamb of God, Son of the Father,
you take away the sins of the world,
   have mercy on us;
you take away the sins of the world,
   receive our prayer;
you are seated at the right hand of the Father,
   have mercy on us.

For you alone are the Holy One,
you alone are the Lord,
you alone are the Most High,
Jesus Christ,
with the Holy Spirit,
in the glory of God the Father.
Amen.

Priest: Let us pray.

The priest invites us to pray. He then says a prayer in the name of all of us, and finishes like this:

Through our Lord Jesus Christ, your Son, who lives and reigns with you in the unity of the Holy Spirit, one God, for ever and ever.

Everyone: Amen.

Glory

With this word, we indicate the greatness of a person. It shows that a person is important. When we say "Glory to God" we are recognizing that God is important in our lives.

Praise

To praise is to speak well and enthusiastically of someone.

Almighty

When we say that God is almighty, we mean that nothing is impossible for God.

Sins of the world

This expression refers to all the evil that is done in the world.

Holy Spirit

This is the Spirit of God, our heavenly guide, who fills us with love for Jesus.

We listen to the Word of God

This is the moment when we listen to several readings from the Bible. We welcome God who speaks to us today.

You can follow the readings in this book. Look for the Sunday that corresponds to today's date.

The first two readings

We sit down for these readings. The first reading is usually taken from the Old Testament. The second is from a letter written by an apostle to the first Christians. Between these two readings, we pray with the responsorial Psalm, which we do best when it is sung.

The Gospel

We stand and sing Alleluia! as we prepare to listen carefully to a reading from one of the Gospels.

Priest: The Lord be with you.

Everyone: And with your spirit.

Priest: A reading from the holy Gospel according to N.

Everyone: Glory to you, Lord.

We trace three small crosses with our thumb: one on our forehead, one on our lips, and another on our heart. When the reading is finished, the priest kisses the book and says:

Priest: The Gospel of the Lord.

Everyone: Praise to you, Lord Jesus Christ.

Homily

We sit down to listen to the comments of the priest, which help us to understand and apply the Word of God in our lives.

Bible

This is the holy book of all Christians. The Old Testament tells the story of the Covenant God made with the Jewish people before Jesus' time. The New Testament tells the story of the Covenant God made with all people through his son, Jesus Christ.

Psalm

The Psalms are prayers that are found in the Bible. They are meant to be sung.

Alleluia!

This Hebrew word means "May God be praised and thanked."

Gospel

The word "gospel" means "good news." Jesus himself is the Good News who lives with us. The first four books of the New Testament are called "Gospels." They transmit the Good News to us.

The sign of the cross which we make on our forehead, lips and heart

means that we want to make the Gospel so much a part of our life that we can proclaim it to all around us with all our heart.

Kissing the book of the Gospels

When the priest does this, he says in a low voice: "Through the words of the Gospel may our sins be wiped away."

We profess our faith

We have just listened to the Word of God. To respond to it, with all other Christians in the world, we proclaim the "Creed."

We stand up and profess our faith:

Everyone: I believe in God,
the Father almighty,
Creator of heaven and earth,
and in Jesus Christ, his only Son, our Lord,
who was conceived by the Holy Spirit,
born of the Virgin Mary,
suffered under Pontius Pilate,
was crucified, died and was buried;
he descended into hell;
on the third day he rose again from the dead;
he ascended into heaven,
and is seated at the right hand
   of God the Father almighty;
from there he will come to judge
   the living and the dead.

I believe in the Holy Spirit,
the holy catholic Church,
the communion of saints,
the forgiveness of sins,
the resurrection of the body,
and life everlasting.
Amen.

What does it mean?

Creed

From the Latin verb *credo* that means "I believe." The Creed is the prayer that expresses our faith as Christians.

He suffered

Means the torture Jesus endured before he died on the cross.

Pontius Pilate

This is the name of the Roman governor who ordered that Jesus be crucified.

Crucified

Jesus died by crucifixion. He was nailed to a cross.

Catholic

In Greek, this word means "universal." The Church is open to all people in the world.

Church

The "Church" with a big C refers to the whole Christian community throughout the world. The "church" with a little c is a building where we gather to worship God.

Resurrection

Means coming back to life after having died. God raised Jesus from the dead and gave him new life for ever. Jesus shares that life with us.

We pray for the whole world

This is the moment of the universal Prayer of the Faithful when we present our petitions to God. We pray for the Church, for all of humanity, for those who are sick or lonely, for children who are abandoned, for those who suffer through natural disasters...

After each petition we respond with a phrase, such as:

Everyone: Lord, hear our prayer.

Reader: For the needs of the Church ...

For peace in every country ...

For the hungry and the homeless ...

For ourselves and for all God's children ...

What does it mean?

Petitions

Petitions are prayers asking for something specific. Each week at Mass, the petitions change because the needs of the world and our community change. We stand for the petitions and answer "Amen" at the end — to show that our prayers are offered as one.

Some questions

Why do we call the Prayer of the Faithful "universal"?

It is a universal prayer because it includes everyone: we pray for all the people of the world.

Why do we take up a collection?

Christians help out with the maintenance of the church building and also help people who are in need. Theses gifts are brought to the altar with the bread and the wine.

We offer bread and wine to God

The celebration of the Lord's Supper continues at the altar. Members of the community bring the bread, the wine, and the gifts collected to relieve the needs of the Church and the poor. The priest presents the bread and wine to God and we bless God with him.

We sit down. The priest takes the bread and wine, and lifts them up, saying:

Priest: Blessed are you, Lord God of all creation, for through your goodness we have received the bread we offer you: fruit of the earth and work of human hands, it will become for us the bread of life.

Everyone: Blessed be God for ever.

Priest: Blessed are you, Lord God of all creation, for through your goodness we have received the wine we offer you: fruit of the vine and work of human hands, it will become our spiritual drink.

Everyone: Blessed be God for ever.

The priest washes his hands and says:

Priest: Pray, brothers and sisters, that my sacrifice and yours may be acceptable to God, the almighty Father.

Everyone: May the Lord accept the sacrifice at your hands for the praise and glory of his name, for our good, and the good of all his holy Church.

We stand while the priest, with hands extended, says a prayer over the bread and wine. He usually ends the prayer by saying:

Priest: Through Christ our Lord.

Everyone: Amen.

What does it mean?

Eucharist

A Greek word that means "gratefulness, thanksgiving." The Mass is also called the Eucharist.

Blessed

To bless means to speak well of someone. To bless God is to give thanks for everything God gives us.

Sacrifice

God does not ask for animal sacrifice, as in the old days. Nor does God ask us to die on a cross, like Jesus did. Instead, God asks us to offer our daily life, with Jesus, as a beautiful gift.

Gestures

Procession with the bread and the wine

With this gesture we present to God the fruit of our work and we give thanks for the gift of life that comes from God.

Drops of water in the wine

With this sign, the priest prays that our life be united with God's life.

Washing of hands

Before saying the most important prayer of the Mass, the priest washes his hands and asks God to wash away his sins.

We give thanks to God

At this moment we give thanks to God for his Son, Jesus Christ, for life, and for all that he gives us. This is how the great Eucharistic Prayer begins.

Priest: The Lord be with you.

Everyone: And with your spirit.

Priest: Lift up your hearts.

Everyone: We lift them up to the Lord.

Priest: Let us give thanks to the Lord our God.

Everyone: It is right and just.

Here is one way of celebrating the Eucharist with young Catholics. On page 21, you will find Eucharistic Prayer II which is a common way of celebrating the Eucharist with grown-ups.

Eucharistic Prayer for Mass with Children I

Priest: God our Father, you have brought us here together so that we can give you thanks and praise for all the wonderful things you have done.

We thank you for all that is beautiful in the world and for the happiness you have given us. We praise you for daylight and for your word which lights up our minds. We praise you for the earth, and all the people who live on it, and for our life which comes from you.

We know that you are good. You love us and do great things for us. So we all sing together:

Everyone: Holy, holy, holy Lord, God of power and might, heaven and earth are full of your glory. Hosanna in the highest.

Priest: Father, you are always thinking about your people; you never forget us. You sent us your Son Jesus, who gave his life for us and who came to save us. He cured sick people; he cared for those who were poor and wept with those who were sad. He forgave sinners and taught us to forgive each other. He loved everyone and showed us how to be kind. He took children in his arms and blessed them. So we all sing together:

Everyone: Blessed is he who comes in the name of the Lord. Hosanna in the highest.

Priest: God our Father, all over the world your people praise you. So now we pray with the whole Church: with N., our pope, and N., our bishop. In heaven the blessed Virgin Mary, the apostles and all the saints always sing your praise. Now we join with them and with the angels to adore you as we sing:

Everyone: Holy, holy, holy Lord, God of power and might, heaven and earth are full of your glory.
Hosanna in the highest.
Blessed is he who comes in the name of the Lord.
Hosanna in the highest.

Priest: God our Father, you are most holy and we want to show you that we are grateful.

We bring you bread and wine and ask you to send your Holy Spirit to make these gifts the body and blood of Jesus your Son. Then we can offer to you what you have given to us.

On the night before he died, Jesus was having supper with his apostles. He took bread from the table. He gave you thanks and praise. Then he broke the bread, gave it to his friends, and said:

Take this, all of you, and eat it:
this is my body which will be given up for you.

The Eucharist

When supper was ended, Jesus took the cup that was filled with wine. He thanked you, gave it to his friends, and said:

> Take this, all of you, and drink from it:
> this is the cup of my blood,
> the blood of the new and everlasting covenant.
> It will be shed for you and for all
> so that sins may be forgiven.

Then he said to them:

> Do this in memory of me.

We do now what Jesus told us to do. We remember his death and his resurrection and we offer you, Father, the bread that gives us life, and the cup that saves us. Jesus brings us to you; welcome us as you welcome him.

Let us proclaim the mystery of faith:

Everyone: Christ has died, Christ is risen, Christ will come again.

Priest: Father, because you love us, you invite us to come to your table. Fill us with the joy of the Holy Spirit as we receive the body and blood of your Son.

Lord, you never forget any of your children. We ask you to take care of those we love, especially of N. and N.; and we pray for those who have died.

Remember everyone who is suffering from pain or sorrow. Remember Christians everywhere and all other people in the world.

We are filled with wonder and praise when we see what you do for us through Jesus your Son, and so we sing:

Through him, with him, in him, in the unity of the Holy Spirit, all glory and honour is yours, almighty Father, for ever and ever.

Everyone: Amen.

(Turn to page 24)

Eucharistic Prayer II

It is truly right and just, our duty and our salvation, always and everywhere to give you thanks, Father most holy, through your beloved Son, Jesus Christ, your Word through whom you made all things, whom you sent as our Saviour and Redeemer, incarnate by the Holy Spirit and born of the Virgin.

Fulfilling your will and gaining for you a holy people, he stretched out his hands as he endured his Passion, so as to break the bonds of death and manifest the resurrection.

And so, with the Angels and all the Saints we declare your glory, as with one voice we acclaim:

Everyone: Holy, Holy, Holy Lord God of hosts.
Heaven and earth are full of your glory.
Hosanna in the highest.
Blessed is he who comes in the name of the Lord.
Hosanna in the highest.

Priest: You are indeed Holy, O Lord, the fount of all holiness. Make holy, therefore, these gifts, we pray, by sending down your Spirit upon them like the dewfall, so that they may become for us the Body and Blood of our Lord Jesus Christ.

At the time he was betrayed and entered willingly into his Passion, he took bread and, giving thanks, broke it, and gave it to his disciples, saying:

> Take this, all of you, and eat of it,
> for this is my Body
> which will be given up for you.

In a similar way, when supper was ended, he took the chalice and, once more giving thanks, he gave it to his disciples, saying:

The Eucharist

Priest:
Take this, all of you, and drink from it,
for this is the chalice of my Blood,
the Blood of the new and eternal covenant,
which will be poured out for you and for many
for the forgiveness of sins.

Do this in memory of me.

The mystery of faith.

Everyone:
We proclaim your Death, O Lord, and profess your Resurrection until you come again.

Priest:
Therefore, as we celebrate the memorial of his Death and Resurrection, we offer you, Lord, the Bread of life and the Chalice of salvation, giving thanks that you have held us worthy to be in your presence and minister to you.

Humbly we pray that, partaking of the Body and Blood of Christ, we may be gathered into one by the Holy Spirit.

Remember, Lord, your Church, spread throughout the world, and bring her to the fullness of charity, together with N. our Pope and N. our Bishop and all the clergy.

Remember also our brothers and sisters who have fallen asleep in the hope of the resurrection, and all who have died in your mercy: welcome them into the light of your face. Have mercy on us all, we pray, that with the Blessed Virgin Mary, Mother of God, with the blessed Apostles, and all the Saints who have pleased you throughout the ages, we may merit to be coheirs to eternal life, and may praise and glorify you through your Son, Jesus Christ.

Through him, and with him, and in him, O God, almighty Father, in the unity of the Holy Spirit, all glory and honour is yours, for ever and ever.

Everyone: Amen.

Covenant

When two people enter into a covenant agreement, they promise to be faithful to one another. God entered into a covenant with us. He is our God and we are his People.

Forgiveness of sins

This is the forgiveness that comes from God, whose love is greater than our sins.

Do this in memory of me

Jesus asked the disciples to remember him by reliving what he said and did during the Last Supper.

The mystery of faith

Together we proclaim our belief in Christ who was born and died for us, rose to life, and will return one day.

Eternal life

This is life with God, which will be given to us fully after death.

Extending the hands

When the priest extends his hands, he calls upon the Holy Spirit to consecrate the bread and wine, so that they become for us the Body and Blood of Christ.

Raising the bread

The priest lifts the consecrated bread and then the chalice, so that the community may see and respectfully adore the Body and Blood of Christ.

Kneeling

This is a common way to show respect and to worship.

The Eucharist

We say the Lord's Prayer

Jesus has taught us that God is the Father of all human beings and that we can call upon God at any time. Together we recite or sing this prayer.

Priest: At the Saviour's command and formed by divine teaching, we dare to say:

Everyone: Our Father,
who art in heaven,
hallowed be thy name;
thy kingdom come,
thy will be done
on earth as it is in heaven.
Give us this day our daily bread,
and forgive us our trespasses,
as we forgive those who trespass against us;
and lead us not into temptation,
but deliver us from evil.

Priest: Deliver us, Lord, we pray, from every evil, graciously grant peace in our days, that, by the help of your mercy, we may be always free from sin and safe from all distress, as we await the blessed hope and the coming of our Saviour, Jesus Christ.

Everyone: For the kingdom,
the power and the glory are yours
now and for ever.

What does it mean?

Saviour

This is one of the names we give to Jesus because he saves us from evil and death.

Heaven

Heaven is a special way of being with God after our life on earth is over.

Kingdom

Jesus speaks of God as king when he says: "The kingdom of God is at hand." With his life, Jesus shows us that God is present in our midst as a king who loves us. When we live as Jesus did, we welcome the kingdom of God.

Trespasses

These refer to our lack of love and to the sins we commit.

Temptation

This is a desire we sometimes feel to do things we know are wrong.

The Eucharist

We share the peace of Christ

God is our Father and we are brothers and sisters in Christ.
In order to show that we are one family, the priest invites us to
offer each other a sign of peace.

Priest: Lord Jesus Christ, who said to your Apostles: Peace I
leave you, my peace I give you, look not on our sins,
but on the faith of your Church, and graciously grant
her peace and unity in accordance with your will.
Who live and reign for ever and ever.

Everyone: Amen.

Priest: The peace of the Lord be with you always.

Everyone: And with your spirit.

Priest: Let us offer each other the sign of peace.

*At this time, by a handshake, a hug or a bow,
we give to those near us a sign of Christ's peace.
Immediately after, we say:*

Everyone: Lamb of God, you take away the sins of the world,
have mercy on us.

Lamb of God, you take away the sins of the world,
have mercy on us.

Lamb of God, you take away the sins of the world,
grant us peace.

What does it mean?

Gestures

Unity

When we get together each Sunday to celebrate the Lord's Supper, we recognize our unity, or oneness, since we are all children of the same loving Father.

Lamb of God

In the Old Testament, believers offered a lamb to God. We call Jesus the Lamb of God because he offers his life to God.

The sign of peace

We shake hands, hug or bow to one another to share the peace that comes from Christ. It is a sign of our commitment to live in peace with others.

We receive Jesus in communion

When we receive communion, the Bread of life, we are fed with the life of Christ.

The priest breaks the host and says:

Priest: Behold the Lamb of God, behold him who takes away the sins of the world. Blessed are those called to the supper of the Lamb.

Everyone: Lord, I am not worthy that you should enter under my roof, but only say the word and my soul shall be healed.

It is time to come up to receive communion. The priest or the communion minister says:

Priest: The Body of Christ.

Everyone: Amen.

Gestures

Why do we go to communion?

When we eat the bread and drink the wine, we receive Jesus. He gives himself to us this way so we can live for God. Sharing the Body and Blood of Christ in communion creates among us a special 'one-ness' with God and with each other.

Why is the bread we share during Mass called a "host"?

The word host means "victim who is offered." The consecrated host is Jesus Christ, who offers himself in order to give life to others.

The priest breaks the bread

The priest breaks the bread in the same way that Jesus did during the Last Supper, in order to share it. The early Christians used to call the Mass "the breaking of the bread."

Receiving the host

The priest or communion minister places the host in your open hand. You eat the bread carefully and return to your place. You take a few moments of quiet prayer to thank God for this Bread of life.

The Lord sends us home

After announcements, the priest blesses us in the name of God. We are then sent to live out our faith among all the people we meet during the week.

Priest: The Lord be with you.

Everyone: And with your spirit.

Priest: May almighty God bless you, the Father, and the Son, and the Holy Spirit.

Everyone: Amen.

Then the priest sends us out, saying:

Priest: Go in peace, glorifying the Lord by your life.

Everyone: Thanks be to God.

What does it mean?

The word "Mass"

The word "Mass" comes from the second word in the Latin phrase that was once used by the priest to announce the end of the Sunday celebration: *Ite missa est* — Go, the Mass is ended.

Communion for the sick

Sometimes people who are sick cannot be present at Sunday Mass. Certain members of the parish, known as communion ministers, can take consecrated hosts to the homes of sick people so that they can receive communion and be assured that the rest of the community is praying for them.

Gesture

Blessing

The priest makes the sign of the cross over the people in church. With this blessing we are sent out with the loving strength of God to live a life of love and service to others.

Dismissal

We cannot stay together in the church all week. When the Mass is ended, we must go our separate ways, in peace and love, to witness to the risen Jesus in the world today.

Liturgical Year

The readings for Sunday Mass and feast days change according to the liturgical calendar.

What is the liturgical year?

Throughout the year, Christians celebrate together important moments in Jesus' life. This is the liturgical year. There are five seasons: Advent, Christmas, Lent, Easter and Ordinary Time.

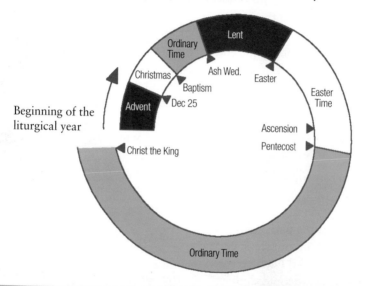

Beginning of the liturgical year

Advent is a time of waiting. It begins 4 weeks before Christmas. We prepare to welcome Jesus.

Christmas season celebrates the life of Jesus from his birth to his baptism. It includes Epiphany: Jesus welcomes the whole world.

During the 40 days of Lent — Ash Wednesday to Holy Saturday — we prepare for the great feast of Easter, the most important moment of the year.

Easter Time is a season to celebrate Jesus' victory over death. It lasts from Easter Sunday to Pentecost, when the Holy Spirit comes upon the disciples.

The season in green above is called Ordinary Time because the Sundays are arranged using 'ordinal numbers.' It recounts many of the things Jesus did and said during his lifetime.

1st Sunday of Advent

You, O Lord, are our father;
"Our Redeemer from of old" is your name.
Why, O Lord, do you make us stray from your ways
and harden our heart, so that we do not fear you?
Turn back for the sake of your servants,
for the sake of the tribes that are your heritage.

O that you would tear open the heavens and come down,
so that the mountains would quake at your presence.
When you did awesome deeds that we did not expect,
you came down, the mountains quaked at your presence.
From ages past no one has heard,
no ear has perceived,
no eye has seen any God besides you,
who works for those who wait for him.

You meet those who gladly do right,
those who remember you in your ways.

But you were angry, and we sinned;
because you hid yourself we transgressed.
We have all become like one who is unclean,
and all our righteous deeds are like a filthy cloth.
We all fade like a leaf,
and our iniquities, like the wind, take us away.
There is no one who calls on your name,
or attempts to take hold of you;
for you have hidden your face from us,
and have delivered us into the hand of our iniquity.

Yet, O Lord, you are our Father;
we are the clay, and you are our potter;
we are all the work of your hand.

The word of the Lord. **Thanks be to God.**

R. **Restore us, O God; let your face shine, that we may be saved.**

Give ear, O Shepherd of Israel,
you who are enthroned upon the cherubim, shine forth.
Stir up your might,
and come to save us. R.

Turn again, O God of hosts;
look down from heaven, and see;
have regard for this vine,
the stock that your right hand has planted. R.

But let your hand be upon the man at your right,
the son of man you have made strong for yourself.
Then we will never turn back from you;
give us life, and we will call on your name. R.

A reading from the first Letter of Saint Paul to the Corinthians (1.3-9)

Brothers and sisters: Grace to you and peace from God our Father and the Lord Jesus Christ.

I give thanks to my God always for you because of the grace of God that has been given you in Christ Jesus, for in every way you have been enriched in him, in speech and knowledge of every kind — just as the testimony of Christ has been strengthened among you — so that you are not lacking in any spiritual gift as you wait for the revealing of our Lord Jesus Christ.

He will also strengthen you to the end, so that you may be blameless on the day of our Lord Jesus Christ. God is faithful; by him you were called into fellowship with his Son, Jesus Christ our Lord.

The word of the Lord. **Thanks be to God.**

Jesus said to his disciples: "Beware, keep alert; for you do not know when the time will come.

"It is like a man going on a journey, when he leaves home and puts his slaves in charge, each with a particular task, and commands the doorkeeper to be on the watch. Therefore, keep awake — for you do not know when the master of the house will come, in the evening, or at midnight, or at cockcrow, or at dawn, or else he may find you asleep when he comes suddenly.

"And what I say to you I say to all: Keep awake."

The Gospel of the Lord. **Praise to you, Lord Jesus Christ.**

With the season of Advent, which means 'coming,' we begin a new liturgical year. Advent lasts four weeks and during this time the liturgical colour is purple. Purple is the colour of waiting; it reminds us to prepare our hearts to celebrate the birth of Jesus at Christmas and his return at the end of time.

To redeem is to buy something back or to pay to free someone. God is called Redeemer because God freed Israel from slavery in Egypt. Christ is our Redeemer, for by his resurrection he freed us from the power of death.

When the Bible says that God has hidden his face, it means that we think God has turned away or is angry. But we know that God is always near and we are the ones who have turned our back to God.

Cherubim (the plural of cherub) are a type of angel. In the Bible they are the ones who watch over the entrance to the Garden of Eden. To show that God is above everything, the psalmist says that God's throne is above the cherubim.

When Saint Paul refers to the day of our Lord Jesus Christ, he is speaking about the end of the world — the day human history will end and we will see God face to face.

The holy Gospel according to Mark is the earliest and the shortest of the four Gospels. The other Gospels were written by Matthew, Luke and John. This year, most of the gospel readings will come from Mark.

2nd Sunday of Advent

Comfort, O comfort my people,
says your God.
Speak tenderly to Jerusalem,
and cry to her
that she has served her term,
that her penalty is paid,
that she has received from the Lord's hand
double for all her sins.

A voice cries out:
"In the wilderness prepare the way of the Lord,
make straight in the desert a highway for our God.
Every valley shall be lifted up,
and every mountain and hill be made low;
the uneven ground shall become level,
and the rough places a plain.
Then the glory of the Lord shall be revealed,
and all people shall see it together,
for the mouth of the Lord has spoken."

Get you up to a high mountain,
O Zion, herald of good tidings;
lift up your voice with strength,
O Jerusalem, herald of good tidings,
lift it up, do not fear;
say to the cities of Judah,
"Here is your God!"

See, the Lord God comes with might,
and his arm rules for him;
his reward is with him,
and his recompense before him.
He will feed his flock like a shepherd;
he will gather the lambs in his arms,
and carry them in his bosom,
and gently lead the mother sheep.

The word of the Lord. **Thanks be to God.**

R. **Show us your steadfast love, O Lord,**
and grant us your salvation.

Let me hear what God the Lord will speak,
for he will speak peace to his people.
Surely his salvation is at hand for those who fear him,
that his glory may dwell in our land. R.

Steadfast love and faithfulness will meet;
righteousness and peace will kiss each other.
Faithfulness will spring up from the ground,
and righteousness will look down from the sky. R.

The Lord will give what is good,
and our land will yield its increase.
Righteousness will go before him,
and will make a path for his steps. R.

A reading from the second Letter of Saint Peter (3.8-14)

Do not ignore this one fact, beloved, that with the Lord one day is like a thousand years, and a thousand years are like one day. The Lord is not slow about his promise, as some think of slowness, but is patient with you, not wanting any to perish, but all to come to repentance.

But the day of the Lord will come like a thief, and then the heavens will pass away with a loud noise, and the elements will be dissolved with fire, and the earth and everything that is done on it will be disclosed.

Since all these things are to be dissolved in this way, what sort of persons ought you to be in leading lives of holiness and godliness, waiting for and hastening the coming of the day of God, because of which the heavens will be set ablaze and dissolved, and the elements will melt with fire? But, in accordance with his promise, we wait for new heavens and a new earth, where righteousness is at home.

Therefore, beloved, while you are waiting for these things, strive to be found by him at peace.

The word of the Lord. **Thanks be to God.**

The beginning of the good news of Jesus Christ, the Son of God.

As it is written in the Prophet Isaiah, "See, I am sending my messenger ahead of you, who will prepare your way; the voice of one crying out in the wilderness: 'Prepare the way of the Lord, make his paths straight,'" John the Baptist appeared in the wilderness, proclaiming a baptism of repentance for the forgiveness of sins. And people from the whole Judean countryside and all the people of Jerusalem were going out to him, and were baptized by him in the river Jordan, confessing their sins.

Now John was clothed with camel's hair, with a leather belt around his waist, and he ate locusts and wild honey. He proclaimed, "The one who is more powerful than I is coming after me; I am not worthy to stoop down and untie the thong of his sandals. I have baptized you with water; but he will baptize you with the Holy Spirit."

The Gospel of the Lord. **Praise to you, Lord Jesus Christ.**

God does not have a body, but to help us understand God, the Bible uses parts of the human body to describe him: God acts (the Lord's hand), God communicates with us (the mouth of the Lord), God is powerful (his arm rules) and God cares for us (gathers us in his arms).

In the second Letter of Saint Peter, the people are worrying about when Jesus will return. Peter helps them understand that the important thing is not to worry but to live well and to let God decide when the Second Coming (or advent) will take place.

Holiness means living near God and letting the Holy Spirit guide us. To be holy is to live in a God-like manner: with love, mercy and compassion.

"Prepare the way of the Lord" were John the Baptist's words to the people, telling them to change their lives so that they would be ready for the Messiah. John the Baptist used the same words as the Prophet Isaiah had done, to show that Jesus was indeed the Promised One, the Messiah.

John the Baptist was the son of Zechariah and Elizabeth (cousin of the Virgin Mary), and therefore Jesus' cousin. He told people that Jesus was coming soon. He was called John the Baptist because he baptized many people.

When we are baptized, we are baptized with water and with the Holy Spirit. We let God into our lives, and the Holy Spirit is alive in us. John the Baptist knew that baptism in the name of Jesus marked the beginning of a new life!

3rd Sunday of Advent

A reading from the book of the Prophet Isaiah
(61.1-2, 10-11)

The spirit of the Lord God is upon me,
because the Lord has anointed me;
he has sent me to bring good news to the oppressed,
to bind up the broken-hearted,
to proclaim liberty to the captives,
and release to the prisoners;
to proclaim the year of the Lord's favour.

I will greatly rejoice in the Lord,
my soul shall exult in my God;
for he has clothed me with the garments of salvation,
he has covered me with the robe of righteousness,
as a bridegroom decks himself with a garland,
and as a bride adorns herself with her jewels.

For as the earth brings forth its shoots,
and as a garden causes what is sown in it to spring up,
so the Lord God will cause righteousness and praise
to spring up before all the nations.

The word of the Lord. **Thanks be to God.**

Luke 1

R. **My soul shall exult in my God.**

My soul magnifies the Lord
and my spirit rejoices in God my Saviour,
for he has looked with favour on the lowliness of his servant.
Surely, from now on all generations will call me blessed. R.

For the Mighty One has done great things for me,
and holy is his name.
His mercy is for those who fear him
from generation to generation. R.

The Lord has filled the hungry with good things
and sent the rich away empty.
He has helped his servant Israel,
in remembrance of his mercy. R.

A reading from the first Letter of Saint Paul to the Thessalonians (5.16-24)

Brothers and sisters, rejoice always, pray without ceasing, give thanks in all circumstances; for this is the will of God in Christ Jesus for you.

Do not quench the Spirit. Do not despise the words of Prophets, but test everything; hold fast to what is good; abstain from every form of evil.

May the God of peace himself sanctify you entirely; and may your spirit and soul and body be kept sound and blameless at the coming of our Lord Jesus Christ. The one who calls you is faithful, and he will do this.

The word of the Lord. **Thanks be to God.**

A reading from the holy Gospel according to John (1.6-8, 19-28)

There was a man sent from God, whose name was John. He came as a witness to testify to the light, so that all might believe through him. He himself was not the light, but he came to testify to the light.

This is the testimony given by John when the Jews sent priests and Levites from Jerusalem to ask him, "Who are you?" He confessed and did not deny it, but confessed, "I am not the Messiah." And they asked him, "What then? Are you Elijah?" He said, "I am not." "Are you the Prophet?" He answered, "No."

Then they said to him, "Who are you? Let us have an answer for those who sent us. What do you say about yourself?" He said, "I am the voice of one crying out in the wilderness, 'Make straight the way of the Lord,'" as the Prophet Isaiah said.

Now they had been sent from the Pharisees. They asked him, "Why then are you baptizing if you are neither the Messiah, nor Elijah, nor the Prophet?" John answered them, "I baptize with water. Among you stands one whom you do not know, the one who is coming after me; I am not worthy to untie the thong of his sandal." This took place in Bethany across the Jordan where John was baptizing.

The Gospel of the Lord. **Praise to you, Lord Jesus Christ.**

To anoint means to 'bless with oil.' In the Bible it can also mean to give someone a mission, an important job. Christians are anointed at baptism and confirmation: our mission is to live as Jesus taught us, bringing good news to the oppressed.

Every 50 years, Israel celebrated a Jubilee Year, a special time when debts were forgiven and wrongs were pardoned. When Isaiah mentions the year of the Lord's favour, he means that, just as in the Jubilee Year, God is offering forgiveness to all those who are sorry for their wrongs and are seeking pardon.

One way to pray is to give thanks to God. We do this, for example, when we say 'grace' before meals — we thank God each day for all the good things God has given us. In many languages, the words for 'grace' and 'thanks' are the same.

Today's Gospel is taken from the holy Gospel according to John, the last of the Gospels to be written. The author of this Gospel was one of the Twelve Apostles. Today we hear of another John — John the Baptist, the cousin of Jesus, who preached that everyone had to change their lives and prepare to receive the Messiah. John the Baptist did not write the Gospel, but he was the greatest of all the prophets.

Jesus, his disciples and the people of the time spoke Aramaic. Messiah is an Aramaic word meaning 'anointed.' The chosen person was anointed or blessed with holy oil and given a special mission. The Greek word for 'anointed' is 'Christ.'

4th Sunday of Advent

Now when David, the king, was settled in his house, and the Lord had given him rest from all his enemies around him, the king said to the Prophet Nathan, "See now, I am living in a house of cedar, but the ark of God stays in a tent." Nathan said to the king, "Go, do all that you have in mind, for the Lord is with you."

But that same night the word of the Lord came to Nathan: "Go and tell my servant David: 'Thus says the Lord: Are you the one to build me a house to live in? I took you from the pasture, from following the sheep to be prince over my people Israel: and I have been with you wherever you went, and have cut off all your enemies from before you; and I will make for you a great name, like the name of the great ones of the earth.

"And I will appoint a place for my people Israel and will plant them, so that they may live in their own place, and be disturbed no more; and evildoers shall afflict them no more, as formerly, from the time that I appointed judges over my people Israel; and I will give you rest from all your enemies.

"Moreover the Lord declares to you, David, that the Lord will make you a house. When your days are fulfilled and you lie down with your ancestors, I will raise up your offspring after you, who shall come forth from your body, and I will establish his kingdom.

"I will be a father to him, and he shall be a son to me. Your house and your kingdom shall be made sure forever before me; your throne, David, shall be established forever.'"

The word of the Lord. **Thanks be to God.**

R. **Forever I will sing of your steadfast love, O Lord.**

I will sing of your steadfast love, O Lord, forever;
with my mouth I will proclaim your faithfulness
    to all generations.
I declare that your steadfast love is established forever;
your faithfulness is as firm as the heavens. R.

You said, "I have made a covenant with my chosen one,
I have sworn to my servant David:
I will establish your descendants forever,
and build your throne for all generations." R.

He shall cry to me, "You are my Father,
my God, and the Rock of my salvation!"
Forever I will keep my steadfast love for him,
and my covenant with him will stand firm. R.

A reading from the Letter of Saint Paul to the Romans (16.25-27)

Brothers and sisters: To the One who is able to strengthen you according to my Gospel and the proclamation of Jesus Christ, according to the revelation of the mystery that was kept secret for long ages but is now disclosed, and through the prophetic writings is made known to all the Gentiles, according to the command of the eternal God, to bring about the obedience of faith — to the only wise God, through Jesus Christ, to whom be the glory forever! Amen.

The word of the Lord. **Thanks be to God.**

The Angel Gabriel was sent by God to a town in Galilee called Nazareth, to a virgin engaged to a man whose name was Joseph, of the house of David. The virgin's name was Mary.

And he came to her and said, "Hail, full of grace! The Lord is with you." But she was much perplexed by his words and pondered what sort of greeting this might be.

The Angel said to her, "Do not be afraid, Mary, for you have found favour with God. And now, you will conceive in your womb and bear a son, and you will name him Jesus.

"He will be great, and will be called the Son of the Most High, and the Lord God will give to him the throne of his father David. He will reign over the house of Jacob forever, and of his kingdom there will be no end."

Mary said to the Angel, "How can this be, since I am a virgin?" The Angel said to her, "The Holy Spirit will come upon you, and the power of the Most High will overshadow you; therefore the child to be born will be holy; he will be called Son of God.

"And now, your relative Elizabeth in her old age has also conceived a son; and this is the sixth month for her who was said to be barren. For nothing will be impossible with God." Then Mary said, "Here am I, the servant of the Lord; let it be done to me according to your word." Then the Angel departed from her.

The Gospel of the Lord.
Praise to you, Lord Jesus Christ.

Samuel, a prophet and judge in Israel, was born over 1,000 years before Jesus. The Lord chose Samuel to anoint the first king of Israel, Saul. Samuel also anointed David, who was king after Saul. The Bible contains two books in his name: 1 Samuel and 2 Samuel.

The ark of God, also called the ark of the covenant, was a wooden box in which the Israelites stored important objects that reminded them that God was their saviour. It was built to contain the two stone tablets on which the Ten Commandments were written, a golden urn of manna (the miraculous bread that fell from heaven when they were living in the desert), and Aaron's staff.

Before he was anointed king of Israel, David was a lowly shepherd. It was by God's grace that David was chosen and not because of anything special David had done to earn the title. When God tells David that "I took you from the pasture," God is reminding him that it is God who chooses, not David.

The holy Gospel according to Luke was written for people who, like Luke, weren't Jewish before becoming Christian. This Gospel tells us the most of what we know of Mary, the mother of Jesus — such as today's wonderful story of the Annunciation.

The Gospel assures us that Joseph was descended from the house of David. This fulfills the promise made by the prophets that the Messiah would be born from among David's descendants. In fact, the Gospel of Matthew opens with a genealogy showing how Jesus is descended from David through Joseph.

Christmas
The Nativity of the Lord

The people who walked in darkness have seen a great light;
those who lived in a land of deep darkness —
on them light has shone.
You have multiplied the nation,
you have increased its joy;
they rejoice before you
as with joy at the harvest,
as people exult when dividing plunder.

For the yoke of their burden,
and the bar across their shoulders,
the rod of their oppressor,
you have broken as on the day of Midian.

For a child has been born for us,
a son given to us;
authority rests upon his shoulders;
and he is named
Wonderful Counsellor, Mighty God,
Everlasting Father, Prince of Peace.

His authority shall grow continually,
and there shall be endless peace
for the throne of David and his kingdom.
He will establish and uphold it
with justice and with righteousness
from this time onward and forevermore.
The zeal of the Lord of hosts will do this.

The word of the Lord. **Thanks be to God.**

R. **Today is born our Saviour, Christ the Lord.**

O sing to the Lord a new song;
sing to the Lord, all the earth.
Sing to the Lord, bless his name;
tell of his salvation from day to day. R.

Declare his glory among the nations,
his marvellous works among all the peoples.
For great is the Lord, and greatly to be praised;
he is to be revered above all gods. R.

Let the heavens be glad, and let the earth rejoice;
let the sea roar, and all that fills it;
let the field exult, and everything in it.
Then shall all the trees of the forest sing for joy. R.

Rejoice before the Lord; for he is coming,
for he is coming to judge the earth.
He will judge the world with righteousness,
and the peoples with his truth. R.

A reading from the Letter of Saint Paul to Titus
(2.11-14)

Beloved: The grace of God has appeared, bringing salvation to all, training us to renounce impiety and worldly passions, and in the present age to live lives that are self-controlled, upright, and godly, while we wait for the blessed hope and the manifestation of the glory of our great God and Saviour, Jesus Christ.

He it is who gave himself for us that he might redeem us from all iniquity and purify for himself a people of his own who are zealous for good deeds.

The word of the Lord. **Thanks be to God.**

In those days a decree went out from Caesar Augustus that all the world should be registered. This was the first registration and was taken while Quirinius was governor of Syria. All went to their own towns to be registered. Joseph also went from the town of Nazareth in Galilee to Judea, to the city of David called Bethlehem, because he was descended from the house and family of David. He went to be registered with Mary, to whom he was engaged and who was expecting a child.

While they were there, the time came for her to deliver her child. And she gave birth to her firstborn son and wrapped him in swaddling clothes, and laid him in a manger, because there was no place for them in the inn.

In that region there were shepherds living in the fields, keeping watch over their flock by night. Then an Angel of the Lord stood before them, and the glory of the Lord shone around them, and they were terrified. But the Angel said to them, "Do not be afraid; for see — I am bringing you good news of great joy for all the people: to you is born this day in the city of David a Saviour, who is the Christ, the Lord. This will be a sign for you: you will find a child wrapped in swaddling clothes and lying in a manger."

And suddenly there was with the Angel a multitude of the heavenly host, praising God and saying, "Glory to God in the highest heaven, and on earth peace among those whom he favours!"

When the Angels had left them and gone into heaven, the shepherds said to one another, "Let us go now to Bethlehem and see this thing that has taken place, which the Lord has made known to us." So they went with haste and found Mary and Joseph, and the child lying in the manger.

The Gospel of the Lord. **Praise to you, Lord Jesus Christ.**

Christmas Day is celebrated on December 25th, but the Christmas season lasts for three weeks, ending with the Baptism of Jesus in January. The liturgical colour for this season is white, the colour of joy and celebration.

Prophets like Isaiah were good men and women who spoke for God. Sometimes their messages were demanding: they asked people to change their lives and attitudes to grow closer to God. At other times, they brought words of comfort.

We sing for joy because our hearts are full of happiness: God has come to be with his people. In today's psalm, we see that all creation — even the trees! — rejoice and glory in the Lord.

A manger is a wooden crate filled with hay to feed the animals in a stable. The baby Jesus was placed in a manger soon after he was born. It was amazing that God would choose to be born in such a simple place.

An Angel of the Lord is a messenger of God. Angels appear many times in the Bible, as we see angels revealing God's plan in the lives of Jesus, Mary and Joseph.

Glory to God in the highest and on earth peace to all people!

Merry Christmas!

Solemnity of Mary,
the Holy Mother of God

A reading from the book of Numbers (6.22-27)

The Lord spoke to Moses: Speak to Aaron and his sons, saying,
Thus you shall bless the children of Israel: You shall say to them,

The Lord bless you and keep you;
the Lord make his face to shine upon you,
and be gracious to you;
the Lord lift up his countenance upon you,
and give you peace.

So they shall put my name on the children of Israel, and I
will bless them.

The word of the Lord. **Thanks be to God.**

Psalm 67

R̷. **May God be gracious to us and bless us.**

May God be gracious to us and bless us
and make his face to shine upon us,
that your way may be known upon earth,
your saving power among all nations. R̷.

Let the nations be glad and sing for joy,
for you judge the peoples with equity
and guide the nations upon earth.
Let the peoples praise you, O God;
let all the peoples praise you. R̷.

The earth has yielded its increase;
God, our God, has blessed us.
May God continue to bless us;
let all the ends of the earth revere him. R̷.

58

A reading from the Letter of Saint Paul to the Galatians (4.4-7)

Brothers and sisters: When the fullness of time had come, God sent his Son, born of a woman, born under the law, in order to redeem those who were under the law, so that we might receive adoption to sonship.

And because you are sons and daughters, God has sent the Spirit of his Son into our hearts, crying, "Abba! Father!" So you are no longer slave but son, and if son then also heir, through God.

The word of the Lord. **Thanks be to God.**

A reading from the holy Gospel according to Luke (2.16-21)

The shepherds went with haste to Bethlehem and found Mary and Joseph, and the child lying in the manger. When they saw this, they made known what had been told them about this child; and all who heard it were amazed at what the shepherds told them.

But Mary treasured all these words and pondered them in her heart.

The shepherds returned, glorifying and praising God for all they had heard and seen, as it had been told them.

After eight days had passed, it was time to circumcise the child; and he was called Jesus, the name given by the Angel before he was conceived in the womb.

The Gospel of the Lord.
**Praise to you,
Lord Jesus Christ.**

The book of Numbers is found in the Hebrew Scriptures or Old Testament. It is called "Numbers" because it talks about many numbers and times when the people of Israel were counted. In Hebrew, it is called "In the Desert", because it tells of the travels of the Israelites, after they left slavery in Egypt.

Moses was a friend of God who was born in Egypt when the Israelites were slaves there. When God asked him to lead the people to freedom, Moses said yes because he loved God and didn't want the people to suffer any more. The people left Egypt on a journey called the 'Exodus' about 1,250 years before the time of Jesus.

Aaron, Moses' older brother, helped him free the Israelites. When Moses went up Mount Sinai to receive God's law, Aaron stayed with the people.

Children of Israel is the name of the people God chose to help everyone in the world know God's love.

To judge with equity is to be fair to everyone. In the psalm, the psalmist is praising God for God's fairness to all people on earth.

Fullness of time means when the time was right for God to send Jesus into the world.

In Aramaic, the language Jesus spoke, Abba means 'Daddy.' By calling God "Abba," Jesus shows that we can talk to God with the same trust and love that small children have for their father.

A manger is the place in a barn or stable for the animals' food. Its name is from the French word *manger*, to eat.

To ponder means to think about something a lot. Like all mothers, Mary remembered all the details surrounding the birth of her child.

Epiphany of the Lord

A reading from the book of the Prophet Isaiah (60.1-6)

Arise, shine, for your light has come,
and the glory of the Lord has risen upon you!
For darkness shall cover the earth,
and thick darkness the peoples;
but the Lord will arise upon you,
and his glory will appear over you.
Nations shall come to your light,
and kings to the brightness of your dawn.
Lift up your eyes and look around;
they all gather together, they come to you;
your sons shall come from far away,
and your daughters shall be carried on their nurses' arms.

Then you shall see and be radiant;
your heart shall thrill and rejoice,
because the abundance of the sea shall be brought to you,
the wealth of the nations shall come to you.
A multitude of camels shall cover you,
the young camels of Midian and Ephah;
all those from Sheba shall come.
They shall bring gold and frankincense,
and shall proclaim the praise of the Lord.

The word of the Lord. **Thanks be to God.**

R. **Lord, every nation on earth will adore you.**

Give the king your justice, O God,
and your righteousness to a king's son.
May he judge your people with righteousness,
and your poor with justice. R.

In his days may righteousness flourish
and peace abound, until the moon is no more.
May he have dominion from sea to sea,
and from the River to the ends of the earth. R.

May the kings of Tarshish and of the isles
render him tribute,
may the kings of Sheba and Seba bring gifts.
May all kings fall down before him,
all nations give him service. R.

For he delivers the needy one who calls,
the poor and the one who has no helper.
He has pity on the weak and the needy,
and saves the lives of the needy. R.

A reading from the Letter of Saint Paul to the Ephesians (3.2-3, 5-6)

Brothers and sisters: Surely you have already heard of the commission of God's grace that was given me for you, and how the mystery was made known to me by revelation.

In former generations this mystery was not made known to humankind as it has now been revealed to his holy Apostles and Prophets by the Spirit: that is, the Gentiles have become fellow heirs, members of the same body, and sharers in the promise in Christ Jesus through the Gospel.

The word of the Lord. **Thanks be to God.**

In the time of King Herod, after Jesus was born in Bethlehem of Judea, wise men from the East came to Jerusalem, asking, "Where is the child who has been born king of the Jews? For we observed his star at its rising, and have come to pay him homage."

When King Herod heard this, he was frightened, and all Jerusalem with him; and calling together all the chief priests and scribes of the people, he inquired of them where the Messiah was to be born. They told him, "In Bethlehem of Judea; for so it has been written by the Prophet: 'And you, Bethlehem, in the land of Judah, are by no means least among the rulers of Judah; for from you shall come a ruler who is to shepherd my people Israel.'"

Then Herod secretly called for the wise men and learned from them the exact time when the star had appeared. Then he sent them to Bethlehem, saying, "Go and search diligently for the child; and when you have found him, bring me word so that I may also go and pay him homage."

When they had heard the king, they set out; and there, ahead of them, went the star that they had seen at its rising, until it stopped over the place where the child was. When they saw that the star had stopped, they were overwhelmed with joy.

On entering the house, they saw the child with Mary his mother; and they knelt down and paid him homage. Then, opening their treasure chests, they offered him gifts of gold, frankincense, and myrrh.

And having been warned in a dream not to return to Herod, they left for their own country by another road.

The Gospel of the Lord.
Praise to you, Lord Jesus Christ.

Epiphany is a Greek word that means 'unveiling,' where something is revealed. God revealed his love for all people by sending us his Son, Jesus, to save us.

Midian, Ephah and Sheba were three ancient kingdoms near Israel. In the book of the Prophet Isaiah in the Bible, they represent all the nations outside Israel.

The Ephesians were a group of Christians in the city of Ephesus. A letter Saint Paul wrote to them is now part of the Bible. Ephesus is located in modern-day Turkey, near the town of Selçuk.

To know something by revelation means that God has shown or given someone this knowledge.

A mystery is something that is very hard to understand. In Saint Paul's letter to the Ephesians, it means God's plan to create a human community in Christ.

Bethlehem of Judea is the city of King David, one of Jesus' ancestors. Joseph and Mary went to Bethlehem for a census (an official counting of all the people). Jesus was born during their stay there. See the map on page 320.

To pay someone homage is to show your respect or honour for them in a public way, such as by bowing or bringing gifts.

Messiah is an Aramaic word meaning 'anointed.' The chosen person was blessed with holy oil and given a special mission. The Greek word for 'anointed' is 'Christ.'

Gold, frankincense and myrrh were three very expensive gifts: gold is a precious metal; frankincense and myrrh are rare, sweet-smelling incenses. Myrrh is the main ingredient in the holy oil used in anointing.

2nd Sunday in Ordinary Time

Samuel was lying down in the temple of the Lord,
where the ark of God was.
Then the Lord called, "Samuel! Samuel!"
and he said, "Here I am!"
Samuel ran to Eli, and said,
"Here I am, for you called me."
But Eli said, "I did not call; lie down again."
So he went and lay down.

The Lord called again, "Samuel!"
Samuel got up and went to Eli, and said,
"Here I am, for you called me."
But he said,
"I did not call, my son; lie down again."
Now Samuel did not yet know the Lord,
and the word of the Lord had not yet been revealed to him.

The Lord called Samuel again, a third time.
And he got up and went to Eli, and said,
"Here I am, for you called me."
Then Eli perceived that the Lord was calling the boy.

Therefore Eli said to Samuel,
"Go, lie down; and if he calls you, you shall say,
'Speak, Lord, for your servant is listening.'"
So Samuel went and lay down in his place.

Now the Lord came and stood there,
calling as before, "Samuel! Samuel!"
And Samuel said, "Speak, for your servant is listening."

As Samuel grew up, the Lord was with him
and let none of his words fall to the ground.

The word of the Lord. **Thanks be to God.**

R. **Here I am, Lord;**
I come to do your will.

I waited patiently for the Lord;
he inclined to me and heard my cry.
He put a new song in my mouth,
a song of praise to our God. R.

Sacrifice and offering you do not desire,
but you have given me an open ear.
Burnt offering and sin offering
you have not required. R.

Then I said, "Here I am;
in the scroll of the book it is written of me.
I delight to do your will, O my God;
your law is within my heart." R.

I have told the glad news of deliverance
in the great congregation;
see, I have not restrained my lips,
as you know, O Lord. R.

A reading from the first Letter of Saint Paul to the Corinthians (6.13-15, 17-20)

Brothers and sisters: The body is meant not for fornication but for the Lord, and the Lord for the body. And God raised the Lord and will also raise us by his power.

Do you not know that your bodies are members of Christ? But anyone united to the Lord becomes one spirit with him. Shun fornication! Every sin that a person commits is outside the body; but the fornicator sins against the body itself.

Or do you not know that your body is a temple of the Holy Spirit within you, which you have from God, and that you are not your own? For you were bought with a price; therefore glorify God in your body.

The word of the Lord. **Thanks be to God.**

John was standing with two of his disciples, and as he watched Jesus walk by, he exclaimed, "Look, here is the Lamb of God!" The two disciples heard him say this, and they followed Jesus.

When Jesus turned and saw them following, he said to them, "What are you looking for?" They said to him, "Rabbi" (which translated means Teacher), "where are you staying?" He said to them, "Come and see." They came and saw where he was staying, and they remained with him that day. It was about four o'clock in the afternoon.

One of the two who heard John speak and followed him was Andrew, Simon Peter's brother. He first found his brother Simon and said to him, "We have found the Messiah" (which is translated the Christ). He brought Simon to Jesus, who looked at him and said, "You are Simon son of John. You are to be called Cephas" (which is translated Peter).

The Gospel of the Lord. **Praise to you, Lord Jesus Christ.**

The ark of God, also called the ark of the covenant, was a wooden box in which the Israelites stored important objects that reminded them that God was their saviour. It was built to contain the two stone tablets on which the Ten Commandments were written, a golden urn of manna (the miraculous bread that fell from heaven when they were living in the desert), and Aaron's staff.

Saint Paul (known then as Saul) was a man who bullied and terrorized the first Christians. One day, he had an experience of the risen Christ vthat changed his whole life. He changed his name to Paul and became a great apostle, travelling to cities all around the Mediterranean Sea, and telling people about the love of Jesus. Several letters he wrote are now in the Bible.

From the moment of our baptism, our body is a temple of the Holy Spirit. Because God lives in us, we should live in a way that honours God.

Jesus paid the price for our freedom. He gave the most valuable thing he had — his life — in order to free us all from sin and death. He chose to do this because he loves us.

To glorify means to give praise. One way we can praise and glorify God is by respecting and taking care of our bodies.

The John mentioned in the Gospel today is John the Baptist. He came before Jesus and had his own followers or disciples. There is another John in the Bible: he is the apostle who wrote today's Gospel.

3rd Sunday in Ordinary Time

The word of the Lord came to Jonah, saying, "Get up, go to Nineveh, that great city, and proclaim to it the message that I tell you." So Jonah set out and went to Nineveh, according to the word of the Lord.

Now Nineveh was an exceedingly large city, a three days' walk across. Jonah began to go into the city, going a day's walk. And he cried out, "Forty days more, and Nineveh shall be overthrown!"

And the people of Nineveh believed God; they proclaimed a fast, and everyone, great and small, put on sackcloth.

When God saw what they did, how they turned from their evil ways, God changed his mind about the calamity that he had said he would bring upon them; and he did not do it.

The word of the Lord. **Thanks be to God.**

Psalm 25

R̂. **Lord, make me know your ways.**

Make me to know your ways, O Lord;
teach me your paths.
Lead me in your truth, and teach me,
for you are the God of my salvation. R̂.

Be mindful of your mercy, O Lord,
and of your steadfast love,
for they have been from of old.
According to your steadfast love remember me,
for the sake of your goodness, O Lord! R̂.

Good and upright is the Lord;
therefore he instructs sinners in the way.
He leads the humble in what is right,
and teaches the humble his way. R̂.

A reading from the first Letter of Saint Paul to the Corinthians (7.29-31)

Brothers and sisters, the appointed time has grown short; from now on, let even those who have wives be as though they had none, and those who mourn as though they were not mourning, and those who rejoice as though they were not rejoicing, and those who buy as though they had no possessions, and those who deal with the world as though they had no dealings with it. For the present form of this world is passing away.

The word of the Lord. **Thanks be to God.**

A reading from the holy Gospel according to Mark (1.14-20)

After John was arrested, Jesus came to Galilee, proclaiming the good news of God, and saying, "The time is fulfilled, and the kingdom of God has come near; repent, and believe in the good news."

As Jesus passed along the Sea of Galilee, he saw Simon and his brother Andrew casting a net into the sea — for they were fishermen. And Jesus said to them, "Come follow me and I will make you fishers of people." And immediately they left their nets and followed him.

As Jesus went a little farther, he saw James son of Zebedee and his brother John, who were in their boat mending the nets. Immediately he called them; and they left their father Zebedee in the boat with the hired men, and followed him.

The Gospel of the Lord.
Praise to you, Lord Jesus Christ.

The book of the Prophet Jonah is the story of a man who lived about 800 years before Jesus. In it, God wants Jonah to be his prophet but Jonah runs away instead. He famously spends three days in the belly of a whale before finally accepting God's word. This story was written to help people understand that God is loving and merciful and never gives up on his people.

Nineveh was the capital of Assyria (today's northern Iraq) in Jonah's time. The people of Israel saw it as a dangerous and evil city because the people there didn't follow God's laws.

To fast means to stop eating for several hours or days. To put on sackcloth means to wear very rough cloth, which irritates the skin. Fasting and putting on sackcloth were signs that people were sorry for their sins and wanted to make their lives better.

When Saint Paul wrote his letter to the Corinthians, Christians thought the world was about to end. Saint Paul says we must change our ways and live as though that day were here — the day we will be with Jesus forever.

To mourn is to feel sad because someone we love has died, or something important is lost. Saint Paul reminds us that a new world is coming very soon, where everything will be good and wonderful, and no one will ever be sad.

To repent means to be sorry for doing something wrong and to change your way of thinking and living for the better. Jesus calls us to repent and to believe in the good news of God's love.

4th Sunday in Ordinary Time

Moses spoke to the people; he said: "The Lord your God will raise up for you a Prophet like me from among your own kin; you shall heed such a Prophet. This is what you requested of the Lord your God at Horeb on the day of the assembly when you said: 'Let me not hear the voice of the Lord my God any more, or ever again see this great fire, lest I die.'

"Then the Lord replied to me: 'They are right in what they have said. I will raise up for them a Prophet like you from among their own kin; I will put my words in his mouth, and he shall speak to them everything that I command him.

"'Anyone who does not heed the words that he shall speak in my name, I myself will hold him accountable. But any Prophet who speaks in the name of other gods, or who presumes to speak in my name a word that I have not commanded him to speak — that Prophet shall die.'"

The word of the Lord. **Thanks be to God.**

Psalm 95

R̶ **O that today you would listen to the voice of the Lord. Do not harden your hearts!**

O come, let us sing to the Lord;
let us make a joyful noise to the rock of our salvation!
Let us come into his presence with thanksgiving;
let us make a joyful noise to him with songs of praise! R̶

O come, let us worship and bow down,
let us kneel before the Lord, our Maker!
For he is our God, and we are the people of his pasture,
and the sheep of his hand. R̶

O that today you would listen to his voice!
Do not harden your hearts, as at Meribah,
as on the day at Massah in the wilderness,
when your ancestors tested me,
and put me to the proof,
though they had seen my work. R̶

Brothers and sisters, I want you to be free from anxieties. The unmarried man is anxious about the affairs of the Lord, how to please the Lord; but the married man is anxious about the affairs of the world, how to please his wife, and his interests are divided.

The unmarried woman and the virgin are concerned about the affairs of the Lord, so that they may be holy in body and spirit; but the married woman is concerned about the affairs of the world, how to please her husband.

I say this for your own benefit, not to put any restraint upon you, but to promote good order and unhindered devotion to the Lord.

The word of the Lord. **Thanks be to God.**

The disciples went to Capernaum; and when the Sabbath came, Jesus entered the synagogue and taught. They were astounded at his teaching, for he taught them as one having authority, and not as the scribes. Just then there was in their synagogue a man with an unclean spirit, and he cried out, "What have you to do with us, Jesus of Nazareth? Have you come to destroy us? I know who you are, the Holy One of God."

But Jesus rebuked him, saying, "Be silent, and come out of him!" And the unclean spirit, convulsing the man and crying with a loud voice, came out of him. They were all amazed, and they kept on asking one another, "What is this? A new teaching — with authority! He commands even the unclean spirits, and they obey him."

At once Jesus' fame began to spread throughout the surrounding region of Galilee.

The Gospel of the Lord.
Praise to you, Lord Jesus Christ.

The people Moses spoke to were the Israelites. He had led them out of slavery in Egypt. At first they did not know how to listen to God and follow his ways. Over time, after many hardships, they learned what it means to be chosen by God and to do God's will.

Thanksgiving means to say thanks. We give thanks to God for every good thing in the world, which comes from him. 'Eucharist' is the Greek word for thanksgiving.

Sheep were very important for the people of Israel: they gave milk, wool and meat. The shepherd had the crucial job of protecting and feeding the sheep; he called them by name and they would follow him. God cares for us like a shepherd cares for his sheep because he loves us. God's powerful hand protects us from harm. We hear his voice and we follow him.

The Sabbath is the day of the week when human beings rest as God did on the seventh day of creation. It is a chance for us to spend time praising God and enjoying creation.

Authority is the power to both say something and do something. Jesus receives his authority from God, his Father. When Jesus tells the unclean spirit to be quiet and come out of the man, it does what he tells it to do.

The word scribe comes from the Latin word for 'to write.' In Jesus' time, scribes wrote letters and kept records for the community. They also studied the Law of Moses. In the gospels, scribes often asked Jesus hard questions. This was how they learned and tested their knowledge of the Law.

5th Sunday in Ordinary Time

A reading from the book of Job

Job spoke to his friends: "Does not the human being have a hard service on earth, and are not their days like the days of a labourer? Like a slave who longs for the shadow, and like a labourer who looks for their wages, so I am allotted months of emptiness, and nights of misery are apportioned to me.

"When I lie down I say, 'When shall I rise?' But the night is long, and I am full of tossing until dawn.

"My days are swifter than a weaver's shuttle, and come to their end without hope. Remember that my life is a breath; my eye will never again see good."

The word of the Lord. **Thanks be to God.**

Psalm 147

R. **Sing praises to the Lord who heals the broken-hearted.**
or **Alleluia!**

How good it is to sing praises to our God;
for he is gracious, and a song of praise is fitting.
The Lord builds up Jerusalem;
he gathers the outcasts of Israel. R.

The Lord heals the broken-hearted,
and binds up their wounds.
He determines the number of the stars;
he gives to all of them their names. R.

Great is our Lord, and abundant in power;
his understanding is beyond measure.
The Lord lifts up the downtrodden;
he casts the wicked to the ground. R.

Brothers and sisters: If I proclaim the Gospel, this gives me no ground for boasting, for an obligation is laid on me, and woe to me if I do not proclaim the Gospel! For if I do this of my own will, I have a reward; but if not of my own will, I am entrusted with a commission. What then is my reward? Just this: that in my proclamation I may make the Gospel free of charge, so as not to make full use of my rights in the Gospel.

For though I am free with respect to all, I have made myself a slave to all, so that I might win more of them.

To the weak I became weak, so that I might win the weak. I have become all things to all people, that I might by all means save some. I do it all for the sake of the Gospel, so that I may share in its blessings.

The word of the Lord. **Thanks be to God.**

As soon as Jesus and his disciples left the synagogue, they entered the house of Simon and Andrew, with James and John. Now Simon's mother-in-law was in bed with a fever, and they told Jesus about her at once. He came and took her by the hand and lifted her up. Then the fever left her, and she began to serve them.

That evening, at sunset, they brought to Jesus all who were sick or possessed with demons. And the whole city was gathered around the door. And he cured many who were sick with various diseases, and cast out many demons; and he would not permit the demons to speak, because they knew him.

In the morning, while it was still very dark, Jesus got up and went out to a deserted place, and there he prayed. And Simon and his companions hunted for him. When they found him, they said to him, "Everyone is searching for you."

He answered, "Let us go on to the neighbouring towns, so that I may proclaim the message there also; for that is what I came out to do." And Jesus went throughout Galilee, proclaiming the message in their synagogues and casting out demons.

The Gospel of the Lord. **Praise to you, Lord Jesus Christ.**

The book of Job is well-known because it talks a lot about why people suffer and where God is when people suffer. It reminds us that even when bad things happen, God is always with us.

A weaver's shuttle is a piece of wood that goes back and forth on a loom, weaving the thread and forming a piece of cloth. An expert weaver can work so fast that sometimes it is hard to see the shuttle. Job says that, like a shuttle, life goes by very quickly.

Long ago, people thought those who acted in strange ways were possessed with demons. By casting out demons, Jesus showed that he had power over what was evil.

To pray is to place ourselves in the presence of God and to listen with our hearts to what God says. Jesus spent many hours praying and he taught his disciples how to pray *(The Lord's Prayer)*. All Christians should take time to pray, alone and with others.

Galilee is a province in the north of Palestine. See the map, page 320. Nazareth, the town where Jesus lived with his parents, is in Galilee, as is the Sea of Galilee, where some of Jesus' disciples worked as fishermen. In Jerusalem, Jesus was known as a Galilean because of his northern accent.

The synagogue is a place where Jews gather to read the Scriptures and pray.

February 12

6th Sunday in Ordinary Time

The Lord spoke to Moses and Aaron, saying: "When someone has on the skin of their body a swelling or an eruption or a spot, and it turns into a leprous disease on the skin of their body, that person shall be brought to Aaron the priest or to one of his sons the priests.

"Anyone who has the leprous disease shall wear torn clothes and let the hair of their head be dishevelled and shall cover their upper lip and cry out, 'Unclean, unclean.' That person shall remain unclean as long as the disease persists; and being unclean, such a one shall live alone with their dwelling outside the camp."

The word of the Lord. **Thanks be to God.**

Psalm 32

R. **You are my refuge, Lord;**
with deliverance you surround me.

Blessed is the one whose transgression is forgiven,
whose sin is covered.
Blessed is the one to whom the Lord imputes no iniquity,
and in whose spirit there is no deceit. R.

I acknowledged my sin to you,
and I did not hide my iniquity;
I said, "I will confess my transgressions to the Lord,"
and you forgave the guilt of my sin. R.

Be glad in the Lord and rejoice, O righteous,
and shout for joy, all you upright in heart. R.

A reading from the first Letter of Saint Paul to the Corinthians (10.31 – 11.1)

Brothers and sisters: Whether you eat or drink, or whatever you do, do everything for the glory of God. Give no offence to Jews or to Greeks or to the Church of God, just as I try to please everyone in everything I do, not seeking my own advantage, but that of many, so that they may be saved. Be imitators of me, as I am of Christ.

The word of the Lord. **Thanks be to God.**

A reading from the holy Gospel according to Mark (1.40-45)

A man with leprosy came to Jesus begging him, and kneeling said to Jesus, "If you choose, you can make me clean." Moved with pity, Jesus stretched out his hand and touched him, and said to him, "I do choose. Be made clean!" Immediately the leprosy left him, and he was made clean.

After sternly warning him Jesus sent him away at once, saying to him, "See that you say nothing to anyone; but go, show yourself to the priest, and offer for your cleansing what Moses commanded, as a testimony to them."

But the man went out and began to proclaim it freely, and to spread the word, so that Jesus could no longer go into a town openly, but stayed out in the country; and people came to Jesus from every quarter.

The Gospel of the Lord.
Praise to you, Lord Jesus Christ.

Leviticus is the third book of the Bible. It describes how the Levites (members of the tribe of Levi) are to celebrate worship in the temple in Jerusalem. It also lists ways these leaders are to keep the community safe and at peace.

Aaron, Moses' older brother, helped him free the Israelites from bondage in Egypt. When Moses went up Mount Sinai to receive God's law, Aaron stayed with the people.

Leprosy, or leprous disease, is a contagious skin disease, known today as Hansen's Disease. In the time of Jesus, this disease could not be cured. People who had leprosy had to live away from their family and others in order to keep the disease from spreading. Jesus is not afraid to touch the leprous man: Jesus heals his body so he can return to his family and friends.

The psalms often speak of God as a refuge: a safe place when there is danger. God is always ready to welcome us with open arms, even when we've been less than perfect.

To give offence is to insult or shock someone by our careless words or actions. Saint Paul wants us to be considerate of other people and do everything for the glory of God.

Jesus said to the man he healed, "Say nothing to anyone," in case people wanted to follow Jesus only to be healed. Jesus hoped people would follow him because of the message he taught: that we are all God's children and God loves us.

7th Sunday in Ordinary Time

Thus says the Lord: "Do not remember the former things, or consider the things of old. I am about to do a new thing; now it springs forth, do you not perceive it? I will make a way in the wilderness and rivers in the desert.

"I will give drink to my chosen people, the people whom I formed for myself so that they might declare my praise.

"Yet you did not call upon me, O Jacob; but you have been weary of me, O Israel! You have burdened me with your sins; you have wearied me with your iniquities.

"I, I am He who blots out your transgressions for my own sake, and I will not remember your sins."

The word of the Lord. **Thanks be to God.**

Psalm 41

R. **Heal me, O Lord,**
for I have sinned against you.

Blessed is the one who considers the poor;
the Lord delivers them in the day of trouble.
The Lord protects them and keeps them alive,
makes them happy in the land,
and does not give them up
to the will of their enemies. R.

The Lord sustains that person on their sickbed;
in their illness you heal all their infirmities.
As for me, I said, "O Lord, be gracious to me;
heal me, for I have sinned against you." R.

But you have upheld me because of my integrity,
and set me in your presence forever.
Blessed be the Lord, the God of Israel,
from everlasting to everlasting. R.

A reading from the second Letter of Saint Paul to the Corinthians (1.18-22)

Brothers and sisters: As surely as God is faithful, our word to you has not been "Yes and No." For the Son of God, Jesus Christ, whom we proclaimed among you, Silvanus and Timothy and I, was not "Yes and No"; but in him it is always "Yes."

For in him every one of God's promises is a "Yes." For this reason it is through him that we say the "Amen," to the glory of God. But it is God who establishes us with you in Christ and has anointed us, by putting his seal on us and giving us his Spirit in our hearts as a first instalment.

The word of the Lord. **Thanks be to God.**

A reading from the holy Gospel according to Mark (2.1-12)

When Jesus returned to Capernaum, it was reported that he was at home. So many gathered around that there was no longer room for them, not even in front of the door; and he was speaking the word to them.

Then some people came, bringing to Jesus a paralysed man, carried by four of them. And when they could not bring him to Jesus because of the crowd, they removed the roof above him; and after having dug through it, they let down the mat on which the paralysed man lay.

When Jesus saw their faith, he said to the man, "Son, your sins are forgiven." Now some of the scribes were sitting there, questioning in their hearts, "Why does this fellow speak in this way? It is blasphemy! Who can forgive sins but God alone?"

At once Jesus perceived in his spirit that they were discussing these questions among themselves; and he said to them, "Why do you raise such questions in your hearts? Which is easier, to say to the paralysed man, 'Your sins are forgiven,' or to say, 'Stand up and take your mat and walk'? But so that you may know that the Son of Man has authority on earth to forgive sins" — he said to the man who was paralysed — "I say to you, stand up, take your mat and go to your home."

And he stood up, and immediately took the mat and went out before all of them; so that they were all amazed and glorified God, saying, "We have never seen anything like this!"

The Gospel of the Lord. **Praise to you, Lord Jesus Christ.**

Isaiah was a prophet of God who lived about 800 years before Jesus. God chose him to help the people of Israel turn back to God. Many of the prophecies about the Messiah are found in the book of the Prophet Isaiah.

Jacob, also called **Israel**, was the son of Isaac, who was the son of Abraham. The twelve tribes of Israel all descended from Jacob.

The **Corinthians** were a community of Christians who lived in Corinth, a city in Greece. Saint Paul wrote them several letters, two of which are in the Bible.

Amen is a Hebrew word that means 'so be it' or 'I know this is true.' By saying Amen after hearing or saying a prayer, we are agreeing with what it says.

Capernaum was a town in Galilee where Jesus spent a lot of time teaching people. At first, they accepted him because he healed many people, but later they became jealous and made him leave.

Blasphemy is a word that insults God. In today's Gospel, the crowd believes that Jesus is being disrespectful of God by claiming that he can forgive sins. In their view, only God can forgive sins. They do not yet realize that Jesus is God.

To **glorify** God means to praise God for all he does for us and help others see God's greatness.

Even now, says the Lord, return to me with all your heart, with fasting, with weeping, and with mourning; rend your hearts and not your clothing.

Return to the Lord, your God, for he is gracious and merciful, slow to anger, and abounding in steadfast love, and relents from punishing.

Who knows whether the Lord will not turn and relent, and leave a blessing behind him: a grain offering and a drink offering to be presented to the Lord, your God?

Blow the trumpet in Zion; sanctify a fast; call a solemn assembly; gather the people. Sanctify the congregation; assemble the aged; gather the children, even infants at the breast. Let the bridegroom leave his room, and the bride her canopy.

Between the vestibule and the altar let the priests, the ministers of the Lord, weep. Let them say, "Spare your people, O Lord, and do not make your heritage a mockery, a byword among the nations. Why should it be said among the peoples, 'Where is their God?'"

Then the Lord became jealous for his land, and had pity on his people.

The word of the Lord. **Thanks be to God.**

R. **Have mercy, O Lord, for we have sinned.**

Have mercy on me, O God, according to your steadfast love;
according to your abundant mercy blot out my transgressions.
Wash me thoroughly from my iniquity,
and cleanse me from my sin. R.

For I know my transgressions,
and my sin is ever before me.
Against you, you alone, have I sinned,
and done what is evil in your sight. R.

Create in me a clean heart, O God,
and put a new and right spirit within me.
Do not cast me away from your presence,
and do not take your holy spirit from me. R.

Restore to me the joy of your salvation,
and sustain in me a willing spirit.
O Lord, open my lips,
and my mouth will declare your praise. R.

A reading from the second Letter of Saint Paul to the Corinthians (5.20 – 6.2)

Brothers and sisters: We are ambassadors for Christ, since God is making his appeal through us; we entreat you on behalf of Christ, be reconciled to God. For our sake God made Christ to be sin who knew no sin, so that in Christ we might become the righteousness of God. As we work together with him, we urge you also not to accept the grace of God in vain. For the Lord says, "At an acceptable time I have listened to you, and on a day of salvation I have helped you." See, now is the acceptable time; see, now is the day of salvation!

The word of the Lord. **Thanks be to God.**

Jesus said to the disciples: "Beware of practising your piety before people in order to be seen by them; for then you have no reward from your Father in heaven.

"So whenever you give alms, do not sound a trumpet before you, as the hypocrites do in the synagogues and in the streets, so that they may be praised by others. Truly I tell you, they have received their reward. But when you give alms, do not let your left hand know what your right hand is doing, so that your alms may be done in secret; and your Father who sees in secret will reward you.

"And whenever you pray, do not be like the hypocrites; for they love to stand and pray in the synagogues and at the street corners, so that they may be seen by others. Truly I tell you, they have received their reward. But whenever you pray, go into your room and shut the door and pray to your Father who is in secret; and your Father who sees in secret will reward you.

"And whenever you fast, do not look dismal, like the hypocrites, for they disfigure their faces so as to show others that they are fasting. Truly I tell you, they have received their reward. But when you fast, put oil on your head and wash your face, so that your fasting may be seen not by others but by your Father who is in secret; and your Father who sees in secret will reward you."

The Gospel of the Lord.
Praise to you, Lord Jesus Christ.

Ash Wednesday marks the beginning of Lent. Ashes are used as a sign of our sorrow for having turned away from God; they are placed on our forehead in the sign of the cross and we wear them until they wear off. The ashes are often produced by burning palms from the previous year's Passion Sunday celebration.

To **rend** something is to tear it apart forcefully. In biblical times, people would tear their clothing and cover themselves with ashes as signs of their repentance. The prophet Joel is saying that God would rather we rend or open our hearts as a sign of our willingness to return to God.

A **congregation** is a gathering of people, usually for worship. In the Hebrew Scriptures, it can also mean the whole people of God.

Ambassadors are messengers who have special authority to deliver a message or speak on someone else's behalf. Saint Paul is telling us that we have a special role to play as followers of Christ: we are chosen to spread the Good News. If we are to be faithful messengers, then we must open our hearts and be reconciled to God.

To be **reconciled** means to be 'at-one' with someone, by making up for something wrong we may have done. Through his death, Jesus makes up for our sins and we are reconciled with God.

The three traditional Lenten practices are prayer, fasting and almsgiving. To give **alms** is to give money to the poor. The word comes from the Greek word for compassion or pity. During Lent, we not only focus on our own spiritual life; we also make a special effort to help those around us who are in need.

Hypocrites are people whose actions don't match their words. They may say they love God, but they don't act in a loving way. Such behaviour hurts that person, others around them, and God.

February 26

1st Sunday of Lent

God said to Noah and to his sons with him, "As for me, I am establishing my covenant with you and your descendants after you, and with every living creature that is with you, the birds, the domestic animals, and every animal of the earth with you, as many as came out of the ark. I establish my covenant with you, that never again shall all flesh be cut off by the waters of a flood, and never again shall there be a flood to destroy the earth."

God said, "This is the sign of the covenant that I make between me and you and every living creature that is with you, for all future generations: I have set my bow in the clouds, and it shall be a sign of the covenant between me and the earth. When I bring clouds over the earth and the bow is seen in the clouds, I will remember my covenant that is between me and you and every living creature of all flesh; and the waters shall never again become a flood to destroy all flesh."

The word of the Lord. **Thanks be to God.**

Psalm 25

R. **Your paths, Lord, are love and faithfulness
for those who keep your covenant.**

Make me to know your ways, O Lord;
teach me your paths.
Lead me in your truth, and teach me,
for you are the God of my salvation. R.

Be mindful of your mercy, O Lord, and of your steadfast love,
for they have been from of old.
According to your steadfast love remember me,
for the sake of your goodness, O Lord! R.

Good and upright is the Lord;
therefore he instructs sinners in the way.
He leads the humble in what is right,
and teaches the humble his way. R.

A reading from the first Letter of Saint Peter (3.18-22)

Beloved: Christ suffered for sins once for all, the righteous for the unrighteous, in order to bring you to God. He was put to death in the flesh, but made alive in the spirit, in which also he went and made a proclamation to the spirits in prison. In former times these did not obey, when God waited patiently in the days of Noah, during the building of the ark, in which a few, that is, eight persons, were saved through water.

Baptism, which this prefigured, now saves you — not as a removal of dirt from the body, but as an appeal to God for a good conscience through the resurrection of Jesus Christ, who has gone into heaven and is at the right hand of God, with Angels, Authorities, and Powers made subject to him.

The word of the Lord. **Thanks be to God.**

A reading from the holy Gospel according to Mark (1.12-15)

After Jesus was baptized, the Spirit drove him out into the wilderness. He was in the wilderness forty days, tempted by Satan; and he was with the wild beasts; and the Angels waited on him.

Now after John was arrested, Jesus came to Galilee, proclaiming the good news of God, and saying, "The time is fulfilled, and the kingdom of God has come near; repent, and believe in the good news."

The Gospel of the Lord. **Praise to you, Lord Jesus Christ.**

We are now in the season of Lent, which began on Ash Wednesday and lasts about 40 days until Easter. During Lent, we pray and reflect on God's great love for us. We prepare our hearts to recall Jesus' suffering and death on the cross. When Lent ends, we celebrate the great feast of Easter, recalling when Jesus rose from the dead.

Genesis is the first book of the Bible. It tells many stories, including the stories of creation, Adam and Eve, the flood, Abraham, and the people's faith in God. These stories help us understand that God loves us and wants us to love him too.

Noah was a good man. God promised to save him, his family and a pair of each animal on earth from the flood that was coming. Noah built a big boat called an ark before the flood came so they could all float safely on the water.

In the book of Genesis, we hear how God made a covenant or promise with his people. From time to time, the people would stray and forget their covenant with God, but God never forgot his promise. God is ever faithful.

After the flood, God put his bow (rainbow) in the sky as a sign of God's promise to love and care for his people forever. Every time we see a rainbow, we can remember God's goodness to all creation.

Satan is one of the names given to the enemy of God and our strongest enemy. Satan works against God and tries to lead people away from God's love. Other names for Satan are the Evil One, Lucifer or the Devil.

March 4

2nd Sunday of Lent

God tested Abraham. He said to him, "Abraham!" And Abraham said, "Here I am."

God said, "Take your son, your only son Isaac, whom you love, and go to the land of Moriah, and offer him there as a burnt offering on one of the mountains that I shall show you."

When Abraham and Isaac came to the place that God had shown him, Abraham built an altar there and laid the wood in order. He bound his son Isaac, and laid him on the altar, on top of the wood. Then Abraham reached out his hand and took the knife to kill his son.

But the Angel of the Lord called to him from heaven, and said, "Abraham, Abraham!" And he said, "Here I am." The Angel said, "Do not lay your hand on the boy or do anything to him; for now I know that you fear God, since you have not withheld your son, your only son, from me."

Abraham looked up and saw a ram, caught in a thicket by its horns. Abraham went and took the ram and offered it up as a burnt offering instead of his son.

The Angel of the Lord called to Abraham a second time from heaven, and said, "By myself I have sworn, says the Lord: Because you have done this, and have not withheld your son, your only son, I will indeed bless you, and I will make your offspring as numerous as the stars of heaven and as the sand that is on the seashore. And your offspring shall possess the gate of their enemies, and by your offspring shall all the nations of the earth gain blessing for themselves, because you have obeyed my voice."

The word of the Lord. **Thanks be to God.**

R. **I will walk before the Lord, in the land of the living.**

I kept my faith, even when I said,
"I am greatly afflicted."
Precious in the sight of the Lord
is the death of his faithful ones. R.

O Lord, I am your servant.
You have loosed my bonds.
I will offer to you a thanksgiving sacrifice
and call on the name of the Lord. R.

I will pay my vows to the Lord
in the presence of all his people,
in the courts of the house of the Lord,
in your midst, O Jerusalem. R.

A reading from the Letter of Saint Paul to the Romans (8.31-35, 37)

Brothers and sisters: If God is for us, who is against us? He who did not withhold his own Son, but gave him up for all of us, will he not with him also give us everything else?

Who will bring any charge against God's elect? It is God who justifies. Who is to condemn?

It is Christ Jesus, who died, yes, who was raised, who is at the right hand of God, who indeed intercedes for us.

Who will separate us from the love of Christ? Will hardship, or distress, or persecution, or famine, or nakedness, or peril, or sword?

No, in all these things we are more than conquerors through him who loved us.

The word of the Lord. **Thanks be to God.**

Jesus took with him Peter and James and John, and led them up a high mountain apart, by themselves. And he was transfigured before them, and his clothes became dazzling white, such as no one on earth could bleach them.

And there appeared to them Elijah and Moses, who were talking with Jesus. Then Peter said to Jesus, "Rabbi, it is good for us to be here; let us make three dwellings, one for you, one for Moses, and one for Elijah." Peter did not know what to say, for they were terrified.

Then a cloud overshadowed them, and from the cloud there came a voice, "This is my Son, the Beloved; listen to him!" Suddenly when they looked around, they saw no one with them any more, but only Jesus.

As they were coming down the mountain, he ordered them to tell no one about what they had seen, until after the Son of Man had risen from the dead. So they kept the matter to themselves, questioning what this rising from the dead could mean.

The Gospel of the Lord.
Praise to you,
Lord Jesus Christ.

God asks Abraham to do something very hard: to sacrifice Isaac, his only son. Even though he didn't understand why he had to do this, Abraham trusted God. Seeing Abraham's faith, God let Isaac live. Isaac eventually had children of his own, including Jacob, the father of the twelve tribes of Israel.

To withhold means to hold back, to give as little as possible. Abraham did not withhold his only son, Isaac, and neither did God. God is very generous: he never holds back, even when it comes to giving his only Son, Jesus.

Offspring are the children that a man and woman bring into the world. Because he trusted in God, Abraham was rewarded with numerous offspring or descendants — the whole people of Israel.

To intercede means to ask for something on behalf of another person. Saint Paul tells us that we can draw strength in difficult times from the knowledge that Jesus intercedes for us with God.

When Jesus was transfigured, he looked different somehow. For a moment, his friends saw who Jesus truly is: the Son of God.

Elijah and Moses lived long before Jesus and were important leaders for the people of Israel. By appearing with them, Jesus is showing that he is the fulfillment both of the prophets (Elijah) and the Law (Moses).

3rd Sunday of Lent

A reading from the book of Exodus (20.1-17)

For the shorter version, omit the indented parts.

God spoke all these words: I am the Lord your God, who brought you out of the land of Egypt, out of the house of slavery; you shall have no other gods before me.

> You shall not make for yourself an idol, whether in the form of anything that is in heaven above, or that is on the earth beneath, or that is in the water under the earth. You shall not bow down to them or worship them; for I the Lord your God am a jealous God, punishing children for the iniquity of parents, to the third and the fourth generation of those who reject me, but showing steadfast love to the thousandth generation of those who love me and keep my commandments.

You shall not make wrongful use of the name of the Lord your God, for the Lord will not acquit anyone who misuses his name.

Remember the Sabbath day, and keep it holy.

> Six days you shall labour and do all your work. But the seventh day is a Sabbath to the Lord your God; you shall not do any work — you, your son or your daughter, your male or female slave, your livestock, or the alien resident in your towns. For in six days the Lord made heaven and earth, the sea, and all that is in them, but rested the seventh day; therefore the Lord blessed the Sabbath day and consecrated it.

Honour your father and your mother, so that your days may be long in the land that the Lord your God is giving you.

You shall not murder. You shall not commit adultery. You shall not steal. You shall not bear false witness against your neighbour. You shall not covet your neighbour's house; you shall not covet your neighbour's wife, or male or female slave, or ox, or donkey, or anything that belongs to your neighbour.

The word of the Lord. **Thanks be to God.**

R. **Lord, you have the words of eternal life.**

The law of the Lord is perfect,
reviving the soul;
the decrees of the Lord are sure,
making wise the simple. R.

The precepts of the Lord are right,
rejoicing the heart;
the commandment of the Lord is clear,
enlightening the eyes. R.

The fear of the Lord is pure,
enduring forever;
the ordinances of the Lord are true
and righteous altogether. R.

More to be desired are they than gold,
even much fine gold;
sweeter also than honey,
and drippings of the honeycomb. R.

A reading from the first Letter of Saint Paul to the Corinthians (1.18, 22-25)

Brothers and sisters: The message about the Cross is foolishness to those who are perishing, but to us who are being saved it is the power of God.

For Jews demand signs and Greeks desire wisdom, but we proclaim Christ crucified, a stumbling block to Jews and foolishness to Gentiles, but to those who are the called, both Jews and Greeks, Christ the power of God and the wisdom of God.

For God's foolishness is wiser than human wisdom, and God's weakness is stronger than human strength.

The word of the Lord. **Thanks be to God.**

The Passover of the Jews was near, and Jesus went up to Jerusalem. In the temple he found people selling cattle, sheep, and doves, and the money changers seated at their tables. Making a whip of cords, he drove all of them out of the temple, both the sheep and the cattle. He also poured out the coins of the money changers and overturned their tables. He told those who were selling the doves, "Take these things out of here! Stop making my Father's house a marketplace!"

His disciples remembered that it was written, "Zeal for your house will consume me."

The Jews then said to him, "What sign can you show us for doing this?" Jesus answered them, "Destroy this temple, and in three days I will raise it up." They then said, "This temple has been under construction for forty-six years, and will you raise it up in three days?" But Jesus was speaking of the temple of his body.

After he was raised from the dead, his disciples remembered that he had said this; and they believed the Scripture and the word that Jesus had spoken.

When he was in Jerusalem during the Passover festival, many believed in his name because they saw the signs that he was doing. But Jesus on his part would not entrust himself to them, because he knew all people and needed no one to testify about human nature, for he himself knew what was within the human person.

The Gospel of the Lord.
Praise to you, Lord Jesus Christ.

The book of Exodus is the second book of the Bible. It tells the story of how God, through Moses, freed his people from slavery in Egypt. God made a promise or covenant with them and gave them the Ten Commandments to show them how to live well.

The Sabbath is the day of the week when human beings rest like God did on the seventh day of creation. It is a chance for us to spend time praising God and enjoying creation.

"You shall not commit adultery" reminds husbands and wives always to be faithful to each other.

Christ is a Greek word that means 'anointed.' The chosen person was blessed with holy oil and given a special mission. The Aramaic word for 'anointed' is 'Messiah.'

The word Gentile refers to anyone who is not Jewish. Saint Paul is called the Apostle to the Gentiles because he taught about Jesus to people who were not Jewish.

The holy Gospel according to John tells us about the life, death and resurrection of Jesus. It was written several years after Jesus died. John's Gospel includes some stories and sayings of Jesus that are not in the other three Gospels (Matthew, Mark and Luke).

Passover is a week-long festival when the Jewish people remember and celebrate that God freed their ancestors from slavery in Egypt. Jesus celebrated the Passover with his friends. In 2012, Passover begins at sundown on April 6.

March 18

4th Sunday of Lent

All the leading priests and the people were exceedingly unfaithful, following all the abominations of the nations; and they polluted the house of the Lord that he had consecrated in Jerusalem.

The Lord, the God of their ancestors, persistently sent his messengers to them, because he had compassion on his people and on his dwelling place; but they kept mocking the messengers of God, despising his words, and scoffing at his Prophets, until the wrath of the Lord against his people became so great that there was no remedy.

Therefore the Lord brought up against them the king of the Chaldeans, who burned the house of God, broke down the wall of Jerusalem, burned all its palaces with fire, and destroyed all its precious vessels. The king took into exile in Babylon those who had escaped from the sword, and they became servants to him and to his sons until the establishment of the kingdom of Persia, to fulfill the word of the Lord by the mouth of Jeremiah, until the land had made up for its Sabbaths. All the days that it lay desolate it kept Sabbath, to fulfill seventy years.

In the first year of King Cyrus of Persia, in fulfillment of the word of the Lord spoken by Jeremiah, the Lord stirred up the spirit of King Cyrus of Persia so that he sent a herald throughout all his kingdom and also declared in a written edict: "Thus says King Cyrus of Persia: The Lord, the God of heaven, has given me all the kingdoms of the earth, and he has charged me to build him a house at Jerusalem, which is in Judah. Whoever is among you of all his people, may the Lord his God be with him! Let him go up."

The word of the Lord. **Thanks be to God.**

R. **Let my tongue cling to my mouth if I do not remember you!**

By the rivers of Babylon —
there we sat down and there we wept
when we remembered Zion.
On the willows there we hung up our harps. R.

For there our captors
asked us for songs,
and our tormentors asked for mirth, saying,
"Sing us one of the songs of Zion!" R.

How could we sing the Lord's song
in a foreign land?
If I forget you, O Jerusalem,
let my right hand wither! R.

Let my tongue cling to the roof of my mouth,
if I do not remember you,
if I do not set Jerusalem
above my highest joy. R.

A reading from the Letter of Saint Paul to the Ephesians (2.4-10)

God, who is rich in mercy, out of the great love with which he loved us even when we were dead through our trespasses, made us alive together with Christ — for it is by grace you have been saved.

And God raised us up with Christ and seated us with him in the heavenly places in Christ Jesus, so that in the ages to come God might show the immeasurable riches of his grace in kindness toward us in Christ Jesus.

For by grace you have been saved through faith, and this is not your own doing; it is the gift of God. This is not the result of works, so that no one may boast. For we are what he has made us, created in Christ Jesus for good works, which God prepared beforehand to be our way of life.

The word of the Lord. **Thanks be to God.**

Jesus said to Nicodemus: "Just as Moses lifted up the serpent in the wilderness, so must the Son of Man be lifted up, that whoever believes in him may have eternal life. For God so loved the world that he gave his only-begotten Son, so that everyone who believes in him may not perish but may have eternal life.

"Indeed, God did not send the Son into the world to condemn the world, but in order that the world might be saved through him. The one who believes in him is not condemned; but the one who does not believe is condemned already, for not having believed in the name of the only-begotten Son of God.

"And this is the judgment, that the light has come into the world, and people loved darkness rather than light because their deeds were evil. For all who do evil hate the light and do not come to the light, so that their deeds may not be exposed. But those who do what is true come to the light, so that it may be clearly seen that their deeds have been done in God."

The Gospel of the Lord.
Praise to you, Lord Jesus Christ.

The two books of Chronicles are part of the Old Testament or Hebrew Scriptures. They focus on the importance of Jerusalem and the temple for the Jewish religion. They tell the story of David, the king of Israel who conquered Jerusalem and made it the centre of the nation.

The abominations of the nations are the actions of non-Jewish people that go against God's law. The worst thing of all is to worship false gods, yet this is what some of God's people did.

The Ephesians were a group of Christians in the city of Ephesus. A letter Saint Paul wrote to them is now part of the Bible. Ephesus is located in modern-day Turkey.

Grace means a gift from God. God gives us this gift so we can live as his children.

When the Israelites wandered through the desert, they encountered poisonous snakes. God told Moses to make a bronze serpent and lift it up on a pole, like a flag. Anyone who was bitten by a snake and looked at the bronze serpent was healed. In today's Gospel, Jesus tells Nicodemus that when he, Jesus, is lifted up on the cross and then raised from the dead, he will bring eternal life to all people who believe in him.

Light is a symbol of all things good and especially of Jesus, who is the Light of the world. Darkness represents evil, especially turning away from God.

March 25

5th Sunday of Lent

The days are surely coming, says the Lord, when I will make a new covenant with the house of Israel and the house of Judah. It will not be like the covenant that I made with their fathers when I took them by the hand to bring them out of the land of Egypt — a covenant that they broke, though I was their husband, says the Lord.

But this is the covenant that I will make with the house of Israel after those days, says the Lord: I will put my law within them, and I will write it on their hearts; and I will be their God, and they shall be my people. No longer shall they teach one another, or say to each other, "Know the Lord," for they shall all know me, from the least of them to the greatest, says the Lord; for I will forgive their iniquity, and remember their sin no more.

The word of the Lord. **Thanks be to God.**

Psalm 51

R. **Create in me a clean heart, O God.**

Have mercy on me, O God,
according to your steadfast love;
according to your abundant mercy
blot out my transgressions.
Wash me thoroughly from my iniquity,
and cleanse me from my sin. R.

Create in me a clean heart, O God,
and put a new and right spirit within me.
Do not cast me away from your presence,
and do not take your holy spirit from me. R.

Restore to me the joy of your salvation,
and sustain in me a willing spirit.
Then I will teach transgressors your ways,
and sinners will return to you. R.

116

A reading from the Letter to the Hebrews (5.7-9)

In the days of his flesh, Jesus offered up prayers and supplications, with loud cries and tears, to the one who was able to save him from death, and he was heard because of his reverent submission. Although he was a Son, he learned obedience through what he suffered; and having been made perfect, he became the source of eternal salvation for all who obey him.

The word of the Lord. **Thanks be to God.**

A reading from the holy Gospel according to John (12.20-33)

Among those who went up to worship at the festival were some Greeks. They came to Philip, who was from Bethsaida in Galilee, and said to him, "Sir, we wish to see Jesus." Philip went and told Andrew; then Andrew and Philip went and told Jesus. Jesus answered them, "The hour has come for the Son of Man to be glorified. Very truly, I tell you, unless a grain of wheat falls into the earth and dies, it remains just a single grain; but if it dies, it bears much fruit. The person who loves their life loses it, and the person who hates their life in this world will keep it for eternal life.

"Whoever serves me must follow me, and where I am, there will my servant be also. Whoever serves me, the Father will honour.

"Now my soul is troubled. And what should I say — 'Father, save me from this hour'? No, it is for this reason that I have come to this hour. Father, glorify your name."

Then a voice came from heaven, "I have glorified it, and I will glorify it again."

The crowd standing there heard it and said that it was thunder. Others said, "An Angel has spoken to him." Jesus answered, "This voice has come for your sake, not for mine. Now is the judgment of this world; now the ruler of this world will be driven out. And I, when I am lifted up from the earth, will draw all people to myself."

Jesus said this to indicate the kind of death he was to die.

The Gospel of the Lord. **Praise to you, Lord Jesus Christ.**

Jeremiah lived about 600 years before Jesus. When he was still very young, God called him to guide the people of Israel back to God. Many people ignored Jeremiah at first and sent him away. But when the people of Israel feared that God had stopped loving them, Jeremiah gave them hope that God would not abandon them.

A covenant is a promise between two people or groups. Although God's people often forgot their covenant, God continued to renew his promise over and over again. In the new covenant through Jesus, God renewed his promise to us and we agree to love one another and God.

At the time of Jeremiah, God's people were divided into two kingdoms: the house of Israel in the north and the house of Judah in the south. Jeremiah announces God's wish for both kingdoms to be united into one nation, under one covenant.

When Jesus says that the time has come for him to be glorified, he is talking about his death. Jesus knows that his path to glory is through a painful death on the cross.

The ruler of this world is Satan — the enemy of God and all people. Satan tries to turn us away from God, but Jesus promises to draw all people to himself and God.

When Jesus says he will be lifted up from the earth, he is talking about when he will rise from the dead to be with God in heaven.

Passion Sunday

An alternate Gospel follows.

A reading from the holy Gospel according to Mark
(11.1-10)

When they were approaching Jerusalem, at Bethphage and Bethany, near the Mount of Olives, Jesus sent two of his disciples and said to them, "Go into the village ahead of you, and immediately as you enter it, you will find tied there a colt that has never been ridden; untie it and bring it. If anyone says to you, 'Why are you doing this?' just say this, 'The Lord needs it and will send it back here immediately.'"

They went away and found a colt tied near a door, outside in the street. As they were untying it, some of the bystanders said to them, "What are you doing, untying the colt?" The disciples told them what Jesus had said; and they allowed them to take it.

Then they brought the colt to Jesus and threw their cloaks on it; and he sat on it. Many people spread their cloaks on the road, and others spread leafy branches that they had cut in the fields.

Then those who went ahead and those who followed were shouting, "Hosanna! Blessed is the one who comes in the name of the Lord! Blessed is the coming kingdom of our father David! Hosanna in the highest heaven!"

The Gospel of the Lord.
**Praise to you,
Lord Jesus Christ.**

or

A reading from the holy Gospel according to John
(12.12-16)

The great crowd that had come to the festival heard that Jesus was coming to Jerusalem. So they took branches of palm trees and went out to meet him, shouting, "Hosanna! Blessed is the one who comes in the name of the Lord — the King of Israel!"

Jesus found a young donkey and sat on it; as it is written: "Do not be afraid, daughter of Zion. Look, your king is coming, sitting on a donkey's colt!"

His disciples did not understand these things at first; but when Jesus was glorified, then they remembered that these things had been written of him and had been done to him.

The Gospel of the Lord. **Praise to you, Lord Jesus Christ.**

A reading from the book of the Prophet Isaiah (50.4-7)

The servant of the Lord said: "The Lord God has given me the tongue of a teacher, that I may know how to sustain the weary with a word. Morning by morning he wakens — wakens my ear to listen as those who are taught. The Lord God has opened my ear, and I was not rebellious, I did not turn backward.

"I gave my back to those who struck me, and my cheeks to those who pulled out the beard; I did not hide my face from insult and spitting.

"The Lord God helps me; therefore I have not been disgraced; therefore I have set my face like flint, and I know that I shall not be put to shame."

The word of the Lord. **Thanks be to God.**

R. **My God, my God, why have you forsaken me?**

All who see me mock at me;
they make mouths at me, they shake their heads;
"Commit your cause to the Lord; let him deliver;
let him rescue the one in whom he delights!" R.

For dogs are all around me;
a company of evildoers encircles me.
My hands and feet have shrivelled;
I can count all my bones. R.

They divide my clothes among themselves,
and for my clothing they cast lots.
But you, O Lord, do not be far away!
O my help, come quickly to my aid! R.

I will tell of your name to my brothers and sisters;
in the midst of the congregation I will praise you:
You who fear the Lord, praise him!
All you offspring of Jacob, glorify him;
stand in awe of him, all you offspring of Israel! R.

A reading from the Letter of Saint Paul to the Philippians (2.6-11)

Christ Jesus, though he was in the form of God, did not regard equality with God as something to be exploited, but emptied himself, taking the form of a slave, being born in human likeness. And being found in human form, he humbled himself and became obedient to the point of death — even death on a cross.

Therefore God highly exalted him and gave him the name that is above every name, so that at the name of Jesus every knee should bend, in heaven and on earth and under the earth, and every tongue should confess that Jesus Christ is Lord, to the glory of God the Father.

The word of the Lord. **Thanks be to God.**

A reading from the Holy Gospel according to Mark
(14.1 – 15.47)

Several readers may proclaim the passion narrative today. N indicates the narrator, J the words of Jesus, and S the words of other speakers. The shorter version begins (page 127) and ends (page 129) at the asterisks.

N   The Passion of Our Lord Jesus Christ according to Mark.

It was two days before the Passover and the festival of Unleavened Bread. The chief priests and the scribes were looking for a way to arrest Jesus by stealth and kill him; for they said,

S   **Not during the festival, or there may be a riot among the people.**

N   While Jesus was at Bethany in the house of Simon the leper, as he sat at the table, a woman came with an alabaster jar of very costly ointment of nard, and she broke open the jar and poured the ointment on his head. But some were there who said to one another in anger,

S   *Why was the ointment wasted in this way? For this ointment could have been sold for more than three hundred denarii, and the money given to the poor.*

N   And they scolded her. But Jesus said,

J   **Let her alone; why do you trouble her? She has performed a good service for me. For you always have the poor with you, and you can show kindness to them whenever you wish; but you will not always have me. She has done what she could; she has anointed my body beforehand for its burial. Truly I tell you, wherever the good news is proclaimed in the whole world, what she has done will be told in remembrance of her.**

N   Then Judas Iscariot, who was one of the twelve, went to the chief priests in order to betray him to them. When they heard it, they were greatly pleased, and promised to give him money. So he began to look for an opportunity to betray him.

On the first day of Unleavened Bread, when the Passover lamb is sacrificed, the disciples said to Jesus,

S   *Where do you want us to go and make the preparations for you to eat the Passover?*

123

N So he sent two of his disciples, saying to them,

J **Go into the city, and a man carrying a jar of water will meet you; follow him, and wherever he enters, say to the owner of the house, "The Teacher asks, 'Where is my guest room where I may eat the Passover with my disciples?'" He will show you a large room upstairs, furnished and ready. Make preparations for us there.**

N So the disciples set out and went to the city, and found everything as he had told them; and they prepared the Passover meal.

   When it was evening, Jesus came with the twelve. And when they had taken their places and were eating, Jesus said,

J **Truly I tell you, one of you will betray me, one who is eating with me.**

N They began to be distressed and to say to him one after another,

S *Surely, not I?*

J **It is one of the twelve, one who is dipping bread into the bowl with me. For the Son of Man goes as it is written of him, but woe to that one by whom the Son of Man is betrayed! It would have been better for that one not to have been born.**

N While they were eating, he took a loaf of bread, and after blessing it he broke it, gave it to them, and said,

J **Take; this is my Body.**

N Then he took a cup, and after giving thanks he gave it to them, and all of them drank from it. He said to them,

J **This is my Blood of the covenant, which is poured out for many. Truly I tell you, I will never again drink of the fruit of the vine until that day when I drink it new in the kingdom of God.**

N When they had sung the hymn, they went out to the Mount of Olives. And Jesus said to them,

J **You will all become deserters; for it is written, "I will strike the shepherd, and the sheep will be scattered." But after I am raised up, I will go before you to Galilee.**

N Peter said to him,

S *Even though all become deserters, I will not.*

J   Truly I tell you, this day, this very night, before the cock crows twice, you will deny me three times.

N   But he said vehemently,

S   *Even though I must die with you, I will not deny you.*

N   And all of them said the same.

They went to a place called Gethsemane; and Jesus said to his disciples,

J   Sit here while I pray.

N   He took with him Peter and James and John, and began to be distressed and agitated. And he said to them,

J   I am deeply grieved, even to death; remain here, and keep awake.

N   And going a little farther, he threw himself on the ground and prayed that, if it were possible, the hour might pass from him.

J   Abba, Father, for you all things are possible; remove this cup from me; yet, not what I want, but what you want.

N   Jesus came and found them sleeping; and he said to Peter,

J   Simon, are you asleep? Could you not keep awake one hour? Keep awake and pray that you may not come into temptation; the spirit indeed is willing, but the flesh is weak.

N   And again he went away and prayed, saying the same words. And once more he came and found them sleeping, for their eyes were very heavy; and they did not know what to say to him.

He came a third time and said to them,

J   Are you still sleeping and taking your rest? Enough! The hour has come; the Son of Man is betrayed into the hands of sinners. Get up, let us be going. See, my betrayer is at hand.

N   Immediately, while he was still speaking, Judas, one of the twelve, arrived; and with him there was a crowd with swords and clubs, from the chief priests, the scribes, and the elders. Now the betrayer had given them a sign, saying,

S   *The one I will kiss is the man; arrest him and lead him away under guard.*

N   So when he came, he went up to Jesus at once and said,

S   "Rabbi!"

N and kissed him. Then they laid hands on him and arrested him. But one of those who stood near drew his sword and struck the slave of the high priest, cutting off his ear. Then Jesus said to them,

J **Have you come out with swords and clubs to arrest me as though I were a bandit? Day after day I was with you in the temple teaching, and you did not arrest me. But let the Scriptures be fulfilled.**

N All of them deserted him and fled.

A certain young man was following Jesus, wearing nothing but a linen cloth. They caught hold of him, but he left the linen cloth and ran off naked.

They took Jesus to the high priest; and all the chief priests, the elders, and the scribes were assembled.

Peter had followed him at a distance, right into the courtyard of the high priest; and he was sitting with the guards, warming himself at the fire.

Now the chief priests and the whole council were looking for testimony against Jesus to put him to death; but they found none. For many gave false testimony against him, and their testimony did not agree. Some stood up and gave false testimony against him, saying,

S *We heard him say, "I will destroy this temple that is made with hands, and in three days I will build another, not made with hands."*

N But even on this point their testimony did not agree. Then the high priest stood up before them and asked Jesus,

S *Have you no answer? What is it that they testify against you?*

N But he was silent and did not answer. Again the high priest asked him,

S *Are you the Christ, the Son of the Blessed One?*

J **I am; and "you will see the Son of Man seated at the right hand of the Power," and "coming with the clouds of heaven."**

N Then the high priest tore his clothes and said,

S *Why do we still need witnesses? You have heard his blasphemy! What is your decision?*

N   All of them condemned him as deserving death. Some began to spit on him, to blindfold him, and to strike him, saying to him,

S   *Prophesy!*

N   The guards also took him over and beat him.

While Peter was below in the courtyard, one of the servant girls of the high priest came by. When she saw Peter warming himself, she stared at him and said,

S   *You also were with Jesus, the man from Nazareth.*

N   But he denied it, saying,

S   *I do not know or understand what you are talking about.*

N   And he went out into the forecourt. Then the cock crowed. And the servant girl, on seeing him, began again to say to the bystanders,

S   *This man is one of them.*

N   But again he denied it. Then after a little while the bystanders again said to Peter,

S   *Certainly you are one of them; for you are a Galilean.*

N   But he began to curse, and he swore an oath,

S   *I do not know this man you are talking about.*

N   At that moment the cock crowed for the second time. Then Peter remembered that Jesus had said to him, "Before the cock crows twice, you will deny me three times." And he broke down and wept.

* * *

N   As soon as it was morning, the chief priests held a consultation with the elders and scribes and the whole council. They bound Jesus, led him away, and handed him over to Pilate. Pilate asked him,

S   *Are you the King of the Jews?*

J   **You say so.**

N   Then the chief priests accused him of many things. Pilate asked him again,

S   *Have you no answer? See how many charges they bring against you.*

N   But Jesus made no further reply, so that Pilate was amazed.

Now at the festival Pilate used to release a prisoner for them, anyone for whom they asked. Now a man called Barabbas was in prison with the rebels who had committed murder during the insurrection. So the crowd came and began to ask Pilate to do for them according to his custom. Then he answered them,

S   *Do you want me to release for you the King of the Jews?*

N   For he realized that it was out of jealousy that the chief priests had handed him over. But the chief priests stirred up the crowd to have him release Barabbas for them instead. Pilate spoke to them again,

S   *Then what do you wish me to do with the man you call the King of the Jews?*

N   They shouted back,

S   *Crucify him!*

N   Pilate asked them,

S   *Why, what evil has he done?*

N   But they shouted all the more,

S   *Crucify him!*

N   So Pilate, wishing to satisfy the crowd, released Barabbas for them; and after flogging Jesus, he handed him over to be crucified. Then the soldiers led him into the courtyard of the palace, (that is, the governor's headquarters); and they called together the whole cohort. And they clothed him in a purple cloak; and after twisting some thorns into a crown, they put it on him. And they began saluting him,

S   *Hail, King of the Jews!*

N   They struck his head with a reed, spat upon him, and knelt down in homage to him. After mocking him, they stripped him of the purple cloak and put his own clothes on him. Then they led him out to crucify him.

They compelled a passer-by, who was coming in from the country, to carry his Cross; it was Simon of Cyrene, the father of Alexander and Rufus. Then they brought Jesus to the place called Golgotha, (which means the Place of a Skull). And they offered him wine mixed with myrrh; but he did not take it. And they crucified him, and divided his clothes among them, casting lots to decide what each should take.

It was nine o'clock in the morning when they crucified him. The inscription of the charge against him read, "The King of the Jews." And with him they crucified two bandits, one on his right and one on his left. Those who passed by derided him, shaking their heads and saying,

S *Aha! You would destroy the temple and build it in three days; save yourself, and come down from the Cross!*

N In the same way the chief priests, along with the scribes, were also mocking him among themselves and saying,

S *He saved others; he cannot save himself. Let the Christ, the King of Israel, come down from the Cross now, so that we may see and believe.*

N Those who were crucified with him also taunted him.

When it was noon, darkness came over the whole land until three in the afternoon. At three o'clock Jesus cried out with a loud voice,

J **Eloi, Eloi, lema sabachthani?**

N which means, "My God, my God, why have you forsaken me?" When some of the bystanders heard it, they said,

S *Listen, he is calling for Elijah.*

N And someone ran, filled a sponge with sour wine, put it on a stick, and gave it to him to drink, saying,

S *Wait, let us see whether Elijah will come to take him down.*

N Then Jesus gave a loud cry and breathed his last.

Here all kneel and pause for a short time.

N And the curtain of the temple was torn in two, from top to bottom. Now when the centurion, who stood facing him, saw that in this way he breathed his last, he said,

S *Truly this man was God's Son!*

* * *

N There were also women looking on from a distance; among them were Mary Magdalene, and Mary the mother of James the younger and of Joses, and Salome. These used to follow him and provided for him when he was in Galilee; and there were many other women who had come up with him to Jerusalem.

When evening had come, and since it was the day of Preparation, that is, the day before the Sabbath, Joseph of Arimathea, a respected member of the council, who was also himself waiting expectantly for the kingdom of God, went boldly to Pilate and asked for the body of Jesus. Then Pilate wondered if he were already dead; and summoning the centurion, he asked him whether he had been dead for some time. When he learned from the centurion that Jesus was dead, he granted the body to Joseph.

Then Joseph bought a linen cloth, and taking down the body, wrapped it in the linen cloth, and laid it in a tomb that had been hewn out of the rock. He then rolled a stone against the door of the tomb. Mary Magdalene and Mary the mother of Joses saw where the body was laid.

Holy Week begins with Passion Sunday, which is also called Palm Sunday. On this day we recall Jesus' arrival in Jerusalem, where people greeted him in the streets shouting joyfully and waving palm branches. During the Gospel, we listen to the whole story of Jesus' last days on earth.

Saint Paul wrote to the Philippians, a community of Christians in Philippi in Greece, when he was in prison. He thanks them for their help and encourages them to keep their faith in Jesus strong.

The name Christ Jesus or Jesus Christ brings together two words: Jesus which means 'God saves,' the name that his parents gave him; and Christ which means 'anointed,' the one chosen by God to be a true prophet, priest and king.

The Passion of Jesus is the story of the last hours of his life. It begins with the Last Supper and ends when his body is placed in the tomb. Passion is a fitting word, for it originally means "suffering."

The festival of Unleavened Bread is part of the Passover feast. For seven days, the Jews eat only unleavened bread with their meals. The bread is baked without leaven, also called yeast, and it comes out flat. Jesus used this kind of bread at the Last Supper.

Each Jewish family prepares a Passover lamb for the festival dinner, when they gather to recall how God freed their ancestors from slavery in Egypt. This follows the instructions that the Angel of God gave to the Israelites, to sacrifice a spring lamb as they prepared to flee Egypt.

The high priest was in charge of the temple in Jerusalem. He and the chief priests could decide if Jesus had broken any of God's laws.

The Resurrection of the Lord
Easter Sunday

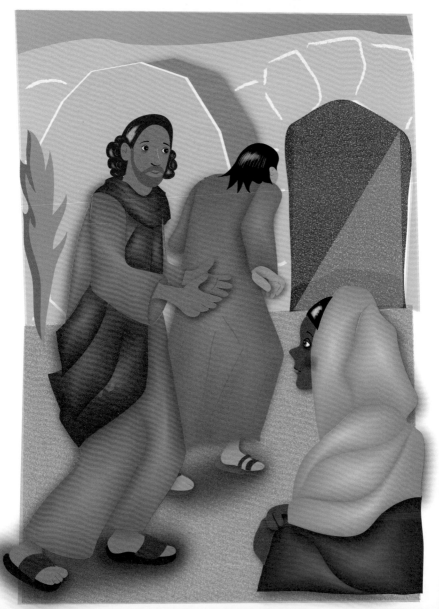

Peter began to speak: "You know the message that spread throughout Judea, beginning in Galilee after the baptism that John announced: how God anointed Jesus of Nazareth with the Holy Spirit and with power; how he went about doing good and healing all who were oppressed by the devil, for God was with him.

"We are witnesses to all that he did both in Judea and in Jerusalem. They put him to death by hanging him on a tree; but God raised him on the third day and allowed him to appear, not to all the people but to us who were chosen by God as witnesses, and who ate and drank with him after he rose from the dead.

"He commanded us to preach to the people and to testify that he is the one ordained by God as judge of the living and the dead. All the Prophets testify about him that everyone who believes in him receives forgiveness of sins through his name."

The word of the Lord. **Thanks be to God.**

Psalm 118

R. **This is the day the Lord has made; let us rejoice and be glad.**

or **Alleluia! Alleluia! Alleluia!**

O give thanks to the Lord, for he is good;
his steadfast love endures forever.
Let Israel say,
"His steadfast love endures forever." R.

"The right hand of the Lord is exalted;
the right hand of the Lord does valiantly."
I shall not die, but I shall live,
and recount the deeds of the Lord. R.

The stone that the builders rejected
has become the chief cornerstone.
This is the Lord's doing;
it is marvellous in our eyes. R.

An alternate reading follows.

A reading from the Letter of Saint Paul to the Colossians (3.1-4)

Brothers and sisters: If you have been raised with Christ, seek the things that are above, where Christ is, seated at the right hand of God. Set your minds on things that are above, not on things that are on earth, for you have died, and your life is hidden with Christ in God. When Christ who is your life is revealed, then you also will be revealed with him in glory.

The word of the Lord. **Thanks be to God.**

or

A reading from the first Letter of Saint Paul to the Corinthians (5.6-8)

Do you not know that a little yeast leavens the whole batch of dough? Clean out the old yeast so that you may be a new batch, as you really are unleavened. For our paschal lamb, Christ, has been sacrificed. Therefore, let us celebrate the festival, not with the old yeast, the yeast of malice and evil, but with the unleavened bread of sincerity and truth.

The word of the Lord. **Thanks be to God.**

A reading from the holy Gospel according to John (20.1-18)

The shorter version ends at the asterisks.

Early on the first day of the week, while it was still dark, Mary Magdalene came to the tomb and saw that the stone had been removed from the tomb. So she ran and went to Simon Peter and the other disciple, the one whom Jesus loved, and said to them, "They have taken the Lord out of the tomb, and we do not know where they have laid him."

Then Peter and the other disciple set out and went toward the tomb. The two were running together, but the other disciple outran Peter and reached the tomb first. He bent down to look in and saw the linen wrappings lying there, but he did not go in.

Then Simon Peter came, following him, and went into the tomb. He saw the linen wrappings lying there, and the cloth that had been on Jesus' head, not lying with the linen wrappings but rolled up in a place by itself. Then the other disciple, who reached the tomb first, also went in, and he saw and believed; for as yet they did not understand the Scripture, that he must rise from the dead.

***

Then the disciples returned to their homes. But Mary Magdalene stood weeping outside the tomb. As she wept, she bent over to look into the tomb; and she saw two Angels in white, sitting where the body of Jesus had been lying, one at the head and the other at the feet. They said to her, "Woman, why are you weeping?" She said to them, "They have taken away my Lord, and I do not know where they have laid him."

When she had said this, she turned around and saw Jesus standing there, but she did not know that it was Jesus. Jesus said to her, "Woman, why are you weeping? Whom are you looking for?" Supposing him to be the gardener, she said to him, "Sir, if you have carried him away, tell me where you have laid him, and I will take him away."

Jesus said to her, "Mary!" She turned and said to him in Hebrew, "Rabbouni!" which means Teacher. Jesus said to her, "Do not hold on to me, because I have not yet ascended to the Father. But go to my brothers and say to them, 'I am ascending

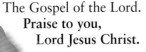

to my Father and your Father, to my God and your God.'"

Mary Magdalene went and announced to the disciples, "I have seen the Lord," and she told them that he had said these things to her.

The Gospel of the Lord.
**Praise to you,
Lord Jesus Christ.**

The Acts of the Apostles is a book in the Bible that describes how the Church grew after Jesus rose from the dead. Written by Luke, who also wrote a Gospel, it mostly tells the story of Peter and Paul.

To anoint means to 'bless with oil.' In the Bible it can also mean to give someone a mission, an important job. Christians are anointed at baptism and confirmation: our mission is to live as Jesus taught us.

God raised him: Jesus' resurrection, his passing through death to eternal life, is the most important element of the Christian faith. We believe that Jesus did not remain dead in the tomb, but overcame death, suffering and sin, and lives now. We want to live as he taught, in order to be united with him now and in the next life.

The Prophets were good men and women who spoke for God. Sometimes their message was harsh: they asked people to make big changes in their lives and attitudes in order to grow closer to God. At other times, they brought words of comfort.

Saint Paul wrote to the Colossians, a Christian community at Colossae in modern-day Turkey, to help them to understand that Jesus Christ is above everything. No powers are greater than he is.

The things that are above, that is in heaven, are those that Jesus teaches: finding the truth, living simply, trusting in God, and caring for those in need. The things of earth distract us from Jesus: being selfish, hurting others and ignoring the poor.

The linen wrappings were the fabric that covered the face of a dead person in the tomb. Joseph of Arimathea and Nicodemus made sure that Jesus' body was buried properly: they wrapped his body in a sheet and covered his face with linen wrappings.

2nd Sunday of Easter

The whole group of those who believed were of one heart and soul, and no one claimed private ownership of any possessions, but everything they owned was held in common.

With great power the Apostles gave their testimony to the resurrection of the Lord Jesus, and great grace was upon them all.

There was not a needy person among them, for as many as owned lands or houses sold them and brought the proceeds of what was sold. They laid it at the Apostles' feet, and it was distributed to each as any had need.

The word of the Lord. **Thanks be to God.**

Psalm 118

R̦. **Give thanks to the Lord, for he is good;
his steadfast love endures forever.**

or **Alleluia!**

Let Israel say,
"His steadfast love endures forever."
Let the house of Aaron say,
"His steadfast love endures forever."
Let those who fear the Lord say,
"His steadfast love endures forever." R̦.

"The right hand of the Lord is exalted;
the right hand of the Lord does valiantly."
I shall not die, but I shall live,
and recount the deeds of the Lord.
The Lord has punished me severely,
but he did not give me over to death. R̦.

The stone that the builders rejected
has become the chief cornerstone.
This is the Lord's doing;
it is marvellous in our eyes.
This is the day that the Lord has made;
let us rejoice and be glad in it. R̦.

A reading from the first Letter of Saint John (5.1-6)

Beloved: Everyone who believes that Jesus is the Christ has been born of God, and everyone who loves the parent loves the child.

By this we know that we love the children of God, when we love God and obey his commandments. For the love of God is this, that we obey his commandments. And his commandments are not burdensome, for whatever is born of God conquers the world. And this is the victory that conquers the world, our faith.

Who is it that conquers the world but the one who believes that Jesus is the Son of God? This is the one who came by water and blood, Jesus Christ, not with the water only but with the water and the blood. And the Spirit is the one that testifies, for the Spirit is the truth.

The word of the Lord. **Thanks be to God.**

A reading from the holy Gospel according to John (20.19-31)

It was evening on the day Jesus rose from the dead, the first day of the week, and the doors of the house where the disciples had met were locked for fear of the Jews. Jesus came and stood among them and said, "Peace be with you." After he said this, he showed them his hands and his side. Then the disciples rejoiced when they saw the Lord.

Jesus said to them again, "Peace be with you. As the Father has sent me, so I send you." When he had said this, he breathed on them and said to them, "Receive the Holy Spirit. If you forgive the sins of any, they are forgiven them; if you retain the sins of any, they are retained."

But Thomas, who was called the Twin, one of the twelve, was not with them when Jesus came. So the other disciples told him, "We have seen the Lord." But he said to them, "Unless I see the mark of the nails in his hands, and put my finger in the mark of the nails and my hand in his side, I will not believe."

After eight days his disciples were again in the house, and Thomas was with them. Although the doors were shut, Jesus came and stood among them and said, "Peace be with you." Then he said to Thomas, "Put your finger here and see my hands. Reach out your hand and put it in my side. Do not doubt but believe." Thomas answered him, "My Lord and my God!"

Jesus said to him, "Have you believed because you have seen me? Blessed are those who have not seen and yet have come to believe."

Now Jesus did many other signs in the presence of his disciples, which are not written in this book. But these are written so that you may come to believe that Jesus is the Christ, the Son of God, and that through believing you may have life in his name.

The Gospel of the Lord. **Praise to you, Lord Jesus Christ.**

The first Christians lived in peace together, sharing their goods, so that what they owned was held in common. A true Christian shares good things for the benefit of all.

Apostle means 'someone who is sent.' This word is used for the twelve close friends who went with Jesus when he was teaching people about God. Jesus later sent them to tell others the good news that God loves us.

When Saint John in his letter speaks of commandments, he means more than the Ten Commandments given to Moses. He also means the greatest commandment — given to us by Jesus — to love one another as Jesus has loved us. All the commandments guide us to love God and everyone we meet along the road of life.

The Holy Spirit is always in our hearts and in the Church, encouraging us to live as children of God. We receive the gifts of the Spirit in the sacraments of baptism and confirmation.

Jesus gave his disciples a very important job: to forgive sins. Today, in the sacrament of reconciliation, God forgives our sins through the priest we talk to. We must also forgive one another.

In John's Gospel, the miracles Jesus performed are called signs. Jesus did these miracles to show or signify that he is the Son of God.

3rd Sunday of Easter

A reading from the Acts of the Apostles (3.13-15, 17-19)

At the temple gate, Peter addressed the people: "The God of Abraham, the God of Isaac, and the God of Jacob, the God of our fathers has glorified his servant Jesus, whom you handed over and rejected in the presence of Pilate, though he had decided to release him.

"But you rejected the Holy and Righteous One and asked to have a murderer given to you, and you killed the Author of life, whom God raised from the dead. To this we are witnesses.

"And now, brothers and sisters, I know that you acted in ignorance, as did also your rulers. In this way God fulfilled what he had foretold through all the Prophets, that his Christ would suffer.

"Repent therefore, and turn to God so that your sins may be wiped out."

The word of the Lord. **Thanks be to God.**

Psalm 4

R. **Let the light of your face shine on us, O Lord.**

or **Alleluia!**

Answer me when I call, O God of my right!
You gave me room when I was in distress.
Be gracious to me, and hear my prayer. R.

But know that the Lord has set apart
the faithful for himself;
the Lord hears when I call to him. R.

There are many who say,
"O that we might see some good!
Let the light of your face shine on us, O Lord!" R.

I will both lie down and sleep in peace;
for you alone, O Lord,
make me lie down in safety. R.

My little children, I am writing these things to you so that you may not sin. But if anyone does sin, we have an advocate with the Father, Jesus Christ the righteous; and he is the atoning sacrifice for our sins, and not for ours only but also for the sins of the whole world.

Now by this we may be sure that we know him, if we obey his commandments. Whoever says, "I have come to know him," but does not obey his commandments, is a liar, and in such a person the truth does not exist; but whoever obeys his word, truly in this person the love of God has reached perfection. By this we may be sure that we are in him.

The word of the Lord. **Thanks be to God.**

A reading from the holy Gospel according to Luke
(24.35-48)

The two disciples told the eleven and their companions what had happened on the road to Emmaus, and how Jesus had been made known to them in the breaking of the bread.

While they were talking about this, Jesus himself stood among them and said to them, "Peace be with you." They were startled and terrified, and thought that they were seeing a ghost. He said to them, "Why are you frightened, and why do doubts arise in your hearts? Look at my hands and my feet; see that it is I myself. Touch me and see; for a ghost does not have flesh and bones as you see that I have."

And when he had said this, he showed them his hands and his feet. While in their joy they were disbelieving and still wondering, he said to them, "Have you anything here to eat?" They gave him a piece of broiled fish, and he took it and ate in their presence.

Then he said to them, "These are my words that I spoke to you while I was still with you — that everything written about me in the Law of Moses, the Prophets, and the Psalms must be fulfilled." Then he opened their minds to understand the Scriptures, and he said to them, "Thus it is written, that the Christ is to suffer and to rise from the dead on the third day, and that repentance and forgiveness of sins is to be proclaimed in his name to all nations, beginning from Jerusalem. You are witnesses of these things."

The Gospel of the Lord. **Praise to you, Lord Jesus Christ.**

144

The God of Abraham, the God of Isaac and the God of Jacob is a name given to the one true God, who had made a covenant with each of these men (also known as the Patriarchs). Peter is telling the Jews that the God of their ancestors, whom they know from the Scriptures, is the one who raised Jesus from the dead. God is with his people!

The first Letter of Saint John was written to the Christian communities in the east. They were disagreeing among themselves, so John wrote to help them sort out their problems.

To sin is to knowingly turn away from God. John tells us in this letter that when we love God, we listen to God and live in a way that is pleasing to God.

The holy Gospel according to Luke was written for people who, like Luke, weren't Jewish before becoming Christian. Luke also wrote the Acts of the Apostles, the book that tells us about the early days of the Christian Church.

On the day Jesus rose from the dead, he walked with two of his disciples back to Emmaus, a village near Jerusalem. They were sad because Jesus was dead. They did not recognize Jesus until he sat down at the table and broke the bread with them, as he had done at the Last Supper.

Breaking of the bread means to celebrate the Lord's Supper, as we do at every eucharist or Mass.

4th Sunday of Easter

While Peter and John were speaking to the people about the resurrection of Jesus, the captain of the temple arrested them and placed them in custody.

The next day the rulers, elders and scribes assembled. When they had made the prisoners stand in their midst, they inquired, "By what power or by what name did you do this?" Then Peter, filled with the Holy Spirit, said to them, "Rulers of the people and elders, if we are questioned today because of a good deed done to someone who was sick and are asked how this man has been healed, let it be known to all of you, and to all the people of Israel, that this man is standing before you in good health by the name of Jesus Christ of Nazareth, whom you crucified, whom God raised from the dead.

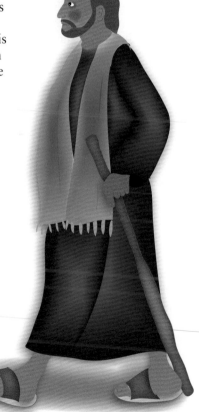

"This Jesus is 'the stone that was rejected by you, the builders; it has become the cornerstone.' There is salvation in no one else, for there is no other name under heaven given among human beings by which we must be saved."

The word of the Lord.
Thanks be to God.

R. **The stone that the builders rejected
has become the cornerstone.**

or **Alleluia!**

O give thanks to the Lord, for he is good;
his steadfast love endures forever!
It is better to take refuge in the Lord
than to put confidence in humans.
It is better to take refuge in the Lord
than to put confidence in princes. R.

I thank you that you have answered me
and have become my salvation.
The stone that the builders rejected
has become the chief cornerstone.
This is the Lord's doing;
it is marvellous in our eyes. R.

Blessed is the one who comes in the name of the Lord.
We bless you from the house of the Lord.
You are my God, and I will give thanks to you;
you are my God, I will extol you.
O give thanks to the Lord, for he is good,
for his steadfast love endures forever. R.

A reading from the first Letter of Saint John (3.1-2)

Beloved: See what love the Father has given us, that we should be called children of God; and that is what we are. The reason the world does not know us is that it did not know him.

Beloved, we are God's children now; what we will be has not yet been revealed. What we do know is this: when he is revealed, we will be like him, for we will see him as he is.

The word of the Lord. **Thanks be to God.**

Jesus said: "I am the good shepherd. The good shepherd lays down his life for the sheep. The hired hand, who is not the shepherd and does not own the sheep, sees the wolf coming and leaves the sheep and runs away — and the wolf snatches them and scatters them. The hired hand runs away because a hired hand does not care for the sheep.

"I am the good shepherd. I know my own and my own know me, just as the Father knows me and I know the Father. And I lay down my life for the sheep. I have other sheep that do not belong to this fold. I must bring them also, and they will listen to my voice. So there will be one flock, one shepherd.

"For this reason the Father loves me, because I lay down my life in order to take it up again. No one takes it from me, but I lay it down of my own accord. I have power to lay it down, and I have power to take it up again. I have received this command from my Father."

The Gospel of the Lord.
Praise to you, Lord Jesus Christ.

Peter is the apostle whose name Jesus changed from Simon, to show how important Peter would be in the life of the Church: 'Peter' means 'rock.' Although Peter let Jesus down by denying him three times when Jesus had been arrested, at other times he showed that he had great faith in Jesus. In today's reading from the Acts of the Apostles, Peter is speaking as the head of the new Christian community.

Elders are leaders or older people who have a great deal of life experience and wisdom. They rely on their experience to help make decisions that benefit everyone.

When Peter says he healed a sick man by using the name of Jesus Christ of Nazareth, he is saying that the power to heal does not come from him, but from Jesus, who is risen from the dead.

The cornerstone of a building is important: it is the stone at the base where two walls meet and therefore supports the whole building. The psalm tells us that what was a worthless stone in the eyes of the builders has become the most important stone of all! Through the resurrection, Jesus has become the cornerstone of our salvation.

A good shepherd is one who feeds his sheep and keeps them safe, day and night. We trust Jesus as sheep trust their shepherd, knowing that God loves us and takes care of us.

The hired hand watches over the sheep because he is paid to do so, but doesn't love them or take risks to protect them. Unlike a hired hand, Jesus will do everything he can to keep us — his sheep — safe.

5th Sunday of Easter

A reading from the Acts of the Apostles (9.26-31)

When Saul had come to Jerusalem, he attempted to join the disciples; and they were all afraid of him, for they did not believe that he was a disciple. But Barnabas took him, brought him to the Apostles, and described for them how on the road he had seen the Lord, who had spoken to him, and how in Damascus Saul had spoken boldly in the name of Jesus.

So Saul went in and out among them in Jerusalem, speaking boldly in the name of the Lord. He spoke and argued with the Hellenists; but they were attempting to kill him. When the believers learned of it, they brought Saul down to Caesarea and sent him off to Tarsus.

Meanwhile the Church throughout Judea, Galilee, and Samaria had peace and was built up. Living in the fear of the Lord and in the comfort of the Holy Spirit, it increased in numbers.

The word of the Lord. **Thanks be to God.**

Psalm 22

℟. **Lord, from you comes my praise in the great congregation.**

or **Alleluia!**

My vows I will pay before those who fear him.
The poor shall eat and be satisfied;
those who seek him shall praise the Lord.
May your hearts live forever. ℟.

All the ends of the earth shall remember and turn to the Lord;
and all the families of the nations shall worship before him.
To him, indeed, shall all who sleep in the earth bow down;
before him shall bow all who go down to the dust. ℟.

I shall live for him.
Posterity will serve him;
future generations will be told about the Lord,
and proclaim his deliverance to a people yet unborn,
saying that he has done it. ℟.

A reading from the first Letter of Saint John (3.18-24)

Little children, let us love, not in word or speech, but in truth and action. And by this we will know that we are from the truth and will reassure our hearts before him whenever our hearts condemn us; for God is greater than our hearts, and God knows everything.

Beloved, if our hearts do not condemn us, we have boldness before God; and we receive from him whatever we ask, because we obey his commandments and do what pleases him.

And this is his commandment, that we should believe in the name of his Son Jesus Christ and love one another, just as he has commanded us. Whoever obeys his commandments abides in him, and he abides in them. And by this we know that he abides in us, by the Spirit that he has given us.

The word of the Lord. **Thanks be to God.**

A reading from the holy Gospel according to John (15.1-8)

Jesus said to his disciples: "I am the true vine, and my Father is the vinegrower. He removes every branch in me that bears no fruit. Every branch that bears fruit he prunes to make it bear more fruit. You have already been cleansed by the word that I have spoken to you.

"Abide in me as I abide in you. Just as the branch cannot bear fruit by itself unless it abides in the vine, neither can you unless you abide in me. I am the vine, you are the branches. Whoever abides in me and I in them bears much fruit, because apart from me you can do nothing.

"Whoever does not abide in me is thrown away like a branch and withers; such branches are gathered, thrown into the fire, and burned.

"If you abide in me, and my words abide in you, ask for whatever you wish, and it will be done for you. My Father is glorified by this, that you bear much fruit and become my disciples."

The Gospel of the Lord. **Praise to you, Lord Jesus Christ.**

Saint Paul's original name was Saul. In the Acts of the Apostles, he is referred to by both names; usually, we think of Saul as who he was before he experienced his conversion and joined the Apostles. Paul is his name as the Apostle to the Gentiles and author of the New Testament letters bearing his name.

Barnabas was an important person in the early Christian community. He was Saint Paul's travelling companion, and was a man of strong faith.

Saint John writes to his friends with affection; that is why he uses the expression little children. He is like a loving grandparent giving advice and encouragement to his grandchildren.

When our hearts condemn us, we know we have done something wrong. Perhaps we have hurt someone else. Our hearts are at ease and we find peace when we repair the damage and ask for forgiveness.

Love one another. With these words, Saint John sums up all of Jesus' teaching and what every Christian must do. He explains that we show love when we help others.

Those who listen to Jesus' words and put them into practice are cleansed. They have put aside the destructive ways of the world; their hearts are pure and full of love.

Branches are the part of the grapevine that produces grapes. If the branch does not bear fruit, it will be pruned or cut away so that the other branches can bear more fruit. By comparing us to branches on a grapevine, Jesus reminds us that our vocation is to share his message of love with others.

To glorify God means to praise, exalt or give glory to him. When we follow Jesus and obey his teaching, we give glory to God.

6th Sunday of Easter

On Peter's arrival, Cornelius, a centurion of the Italian cohort, met him, and falling at his feet, worshipped him. But Peter made him get up, saying, "Stand up; I am only a man."

Then Peter began to speak, "I truly understand that God shows no partiality, but in every nation anyone who fears him and does what is right is acceptable to him."

While Peter was still speaking, the Holy Spirit fell upon all who heard the word. The circumcised believers who had come with Peter were astounded that the gift of the Holy Spirit had been poured out even on the Gentiles, for they heard them speaking in tongues and extolling God.

Then Peter said, "Can anyone withhold the water for baptizing these people who have received the Holy Spirit just as we have?" So he ordered them to be baptized in the name of Jesus Christ. Then they invited him to stay for several days.

The word of the Lord. **Thanks be to God.**

Psalm 98

R. **The Lord has revealed his victory in the sight of the nations.**

or **Alleluia!**

O sing to the Lord a new song,
for he has done marvellous things.
His right hand and his holy arm
have brought him victory. R.

The Lord has made known his victory;
he has revealed his vindication in the sight of the nations.
He has remembered his steadfast love
and faithfulness to the house of Israel. R.

All the ends of the earth have seen
the victory of our God.
Make a joyful noise to the Lord, all the earth;
break forth into joyous song and sing praises. R.

A reading from the first Letter of Saint John (4.7-10)

Beloved, let us love one another, because love is from God; everyone who loves is born of God and knows God. Whoever does not love does not know God, for God is love.

God's love was revealed among us in this way: God sent his only-begotten Son into the world so that we might live through him. In this is love, not that we loved God but that he loved us and sent his Son to be the atoning sacrifice for our sins.

The word of the Lord. **Thanks be to God.**

A reading from the holy Gospel according to John (15.9-17)

Jesus said to his disciples: "As the Father has loved me, so I have loved you; abide in my love. If you keep my commandments, you will abide in my love, just as I have kept my Father's commandments and abide in his love.

"I have said these things to you so that my joy may be in you, and that your joy may be complete. This is my commandment, that you love one another as I have loved you. No one has greater love than this, to lay down one's life for one's friends.

"You are my friends if you do what I command you. I do not call you servants any longer, because the servant does not know what the master is doing; but I have called you friends, because I have made known to you everything that I have heard from my Father.

"You did not choose me but I chose you. And I appointed you to go and bear fruit, fruit that will last, so that the Father will give you whatever you ask him in my name. I am giving you these commands so that you may love one another."

The Gospel of the Lord. **Praise to you, Lord Jesus Christ.**

At the time of Jesus, a Roman army or legion consisted of ten cohorts or units. Each cohort was made up of six smaller units called centuria; a centurion was the Roman military officer who was in charge of a centuria. It is because Cornelius was a senior Roman military officer, and the Romans were the occupying force at the time, that Cornelius' actions are so remarkable.

To show partiality is to be nice to one person and not another. God is impartial and treats everyone the same way: with love.

To atone is to make up for something wrong we have done: it originally meant to be 'at one' or reconciled. Jesus is the atoning sacrifice for our sins: through his death our sins are forgiven and we have eternal life.

Many things can bring us joy: for example, good health, loyal friends and peace in our family. Jesus tells us that our greatest joy is to love others as he has loved us. When we do this, his joy will be with us and we will be 'at one' with Jesus.

We bear fruit when we spread Jesus' message of love wherever we go and in all we do.

Ascension of the Lord

In the first book, Theophilus, I wrote about all that Jesus did and taught from the beginning until the day when he was taken up to heaven, after giving instructions through the Holy Spirit to the Apostles whom he had chosen. After his suffering he presented himself alive to them by many convincing proofs, appearing to them during forty days and speaking about the kingdom of God.

While staying with them, he ordered them not to leave Jerusalem, but to wait there for the promise of the Father. "This," he said, "is what you have heard from me; for John baptized with water, but you will be baptized with the Holy Spirit not many days from now."

So when they had come together, they asked him, "Lord, is this the time when you will restore the kingdom to Israel?" He replied, "It is not for you to know the times or periods that the Father has set by his own authority. But you will receive power when the Holy Spirit has come upon you; and you will be my witnesses in Jerusalem, in all Judea and Samaria, and to the ends of the earth."

When he had said this, as they were watching, he was lifted up, and a cloud took him out of their sight. While he was going and they were gazing up toward heaven, suddenly two men in white robes stood by them. They said, "Men of Galilee, why do you stand looking up toward heaven? This Jesus, who has been taken up from you into heaven, will come in the same way as you saw him go into heaven."

The word of the Lord. **Thanks be to God.**

R̸ **God has gone up with a shout,**
the Lord with the sound of a trumpet.

or **Alleluia!**

Clap your hands, all you peoples;
shout to God with loud songs of joy.
For the Lord, the Most High, is awesome,
a great king over all the earth. R̸

God has gone up with a shout,
the Lord with the sound of a trumpet.
Sing praises to God, sing praises;
sing praises to our King, sing praises. R̸

For God is the king of all the earth;
sing praises with a Psalm.
God is king over the nations;
God sits on his holy throne. R̸

An alternate reading follows.

A reading from the Letter of Saint Paul to the Ephesians (1.17-23)

Brothers and sisters: I pray that the God of our Lord Jesus Christ, the Father of glory, may give you a spirit of wisdom and revelation as you come to know him, so that, with the eyes of your heart enlightened, you may know what is the hope to which he has called you, what are the riches of his glorious inheritance among the saints, and what is the immeasurable greatness of his power for us who believe, according to the working of his great power.

God put this power to work in Christ when he raised him from the dead and seated him at his right hand in the heavenly places, far above all rule and authority and power and dominion, and above every name that is named, not only in this age but also in the age to come.

And he has put all things under his feet and has made him the head over all things for the Church, which is his body, the fullness of him who fills all in all.

The word of the Lord. **Thanks be to God.**

or

A reading from the Letter of Saint Paul to the Ephesians (4.1-13)

For the shorter version, omit the indented part.

Brothers and sisters: I, the prisoner in the Lord, beg you to lead a life worthy of the calling to which you have been called, with all humility and gentleness, with patience, bearing with one another in love, making every effort to maintain the unity of the Spirit in the bond of peace.

There is one body and one Spirit, just as you were called to the one hope of your calling, one Lord, one faith, one baptism, one God and Father of all, who is above all and through all and in all. But each of us was given grace according to the measure of Christ's gift.

> Therefore it is said, "When he ascended on high he made captivity itself a captive; he gave gifts to his people."
>
> When it says, "He ascended," what does it mean but that he had also descended into the lower parts of the earth?
>
> He who descended is the same one who ascended far above all the heavens, so that he might fill all things.

The gifts he gave were that some would be Apostles, some Prophets, some evangelists, some pastors and teachers, to equip the saints for the work of ministry, for building up the body of Christ, until all of us come to the unity of the faith and of the knowledge of the Son of God, to maturity, to the measure of the full stature of Christ.

The word of the Lord. **Thanks be to God.**

Jesus appeared to the eleven, and he said to them, "Go into all the world and proclaim the good news to the whole creation. The one who believes and is baptized will be saved; but the one who does not believe will be condemned. And these signs will accompany those who believe: by using my name they will cast out demons; they will speak in new tongues; they will pick up snakes in their hands, and if they drink any deadly thing, it will not hurt them; they will lay their hands on the sick, and they will recover."

So then the Lord Jesus, after he had spoken to them, was taken up into heaven and sat down at the right hand of God. And they went out and proclaimed the good news everywhere, while the Lord worked with them and confirmed the message by the signs that accompanied it.

The Gospel of the Lord.
**Praise to you,
Lord Jesus Christ.**

KEY WORDS

Saint Luke is the author of the Acts of the Apostles, in addition to the Gospel according to Luke. He addresses the Acts of the Apostles to Theophilus, a name that can mean any one of us: Theophilus is Greek for 'friend of God' or 'beloved by God.'

In the Bible, the expression kingdom of God describes a way of living as God asks. To enter into the kingdom means to live as children of God, our Father, to do his will, and to gain eternal life.

People who are baptized with the Holy Spirit have let God into their lives. The Holy Spirit is alive in them. The apostles received the Holy Spirit on the day of Pentecost. We receive the Holy Spirit in the sacraments of baptism and confirmation.

The Ascension of the Lord is the feast day when we remember how the risen Christ said goodbye to his disciples and was lifted up (ascended) to heaven. Jesus is still with us in spirit, but his resurrected body is with the Father. Each Sunday at Mass we celebrate Jesus who is present among us.

The eleven are the apostles of Jesus. They were twelve at first, but Judas Iscariot, who betrayed Jesus, left before Jesus died, leaving eleven followers after the resurrection. Soon after, the group elected Matthias to replace Judas.

The good news refers to the message of Jesus: that God loves us and wants us to live with him forever.

The position of greatest importance next to a king is the seat at his right hand. When Saint Mark tells us Jesus sat down at the right hand of God, he is a saying that Jesus is very close to God the Father.

Pentecost Sunday

When the day of Pentecost had come, they were all together in one place. And suddenly from heaven there came a sound like the rush of a violent wind, and it filled the entire house where they were sitting. Divided tongues, as of fire, appeared among them, and a tongue rested on each of them. All of them were filled with the Holy Spirit and began to speak in other languages, as the Spirit gave them ability.

Now there were devout Jews from every nation under heaven living in Jerusalem. And at this sound the crowd gathered and was bewildered, because each one heard them speaking in their own language. Amazed and astonished, they asked, "Are not all these who are speaking Galileans? And how is it that we hear, each of us, in our own language? Parthians, Medes, Elamites, and residents of Mesopotamia, Judea and Cappadocia, Pontus and Asia, Phrygia and Pamphylia, Egypt and the parts of Libya belonging to Cyrene, and visitors from Rome, both Jews and converts, Cretans and Arabs — in our own languages we hear them speaking about God's deeds of power."

The word of the Lord. **Thanks be to God.**

Psalm 104

R. **Lord, send forth your Spirit,
and renew the face of the earth.**

or **Alleluia!**

Bless the Lord, O my soul.
O Lord my God, you are very great.
O Lord, how manifold are your works!
the earth is full of your creatures. R.

When you take away their breath,
they die and return to their dust.
When you send forth your spirit, they are created;
and you renew the face of the earth. R.

May the glory of the Lord endure forever;
may the Lord rejoice in his works.
May my meditation be pleasing to him,
for I rejoice in the Lord. R.

An alternate reading follows.

A reading from the first Letter of Saint Paul to the Corinthians (12.3-7, 12-13)

Brothers and sisters: No one can say "Jesus is Lord" except by the Holy Spirit.

Now there are varieties of gifts, but the same Spirit; and there are varieties of services, but the same Lord; and there are varieties of activities, but it is the same God who activates all of them in everyone. To each is given the manifestation of the Spirit for the common good.

For just as the body is one and has many members, and all the members of the body, though many, are one body, so it is with Christ. For in the one Spirit we were all baptized into one body — Jews or Greeks, slaves or free — and we were all made to drink of one Spirit.

The word of the Lord. **Thanks be to God.**

or

A reading from the Letter of Saint Paul to the Galatians (5.16-25)

Brothers and sisters: Live by the Spirit, I say, and do not gratify the desires of the flesh. For what the flesh desires is opposed to the Spirit, and what the Spirit desires is opposed to the flesh; for these are opposed to each other, to prevent you from doing what you want.

But if you are led by the Spirit, you are not subject to the law. Now the works of the flesh are obvious: fornication, impurity, licentiousness, idolatry, sorcery, enmities, strife, jealousy, anger, quarrels, dissensions, factions, envy, drunkenness, carousing, and things like these. I am warning you, as I warned you before: those who do such things will not inherit the kingdom of God.

By contrast, the fruit of the Spirit is love, joy, peace, patience, kindness, generosity, faithfulness, gentleness, and self-control. There is no law against such things. And those who belong to Christ Jesus have crucified the flesh with its passions and desires. If we live by the Spirit, let us also be guided by the Spirit.

The word of the Lord. **Thanks be to God.**

An alternate Gospel follows.

A reading from the holy Gospel according to John
(20.19-23)

It was evening on the day Jesus rose from the dead, the first day of the week, and the doors of the house where the disciples had met were locked for fear of the Jews. Jesus came and stood among them and said, "Peace be with you." After he said this, he showed them his hands and his side. Then the disciples rejoiced when they saw the Lord.

Jesus said to them again, "Peace be with you. As the Father has sent me, so I send you."

When he had said this, he breathed on them and said to them, "Receive the Holy Spirit. If you forgive the sins of any, they are forgiven them; if you retain the sins of any, they are retained."

The Gospel of the Lord. **Praise to you, Lord Jesus Christ.**

or

A reading from the holy Gospel according to John
(15.26-27; 16.12-15)

Jesus said to the disciples: "When the Advocate comes, whom I will send to you from the Father, the Spirit of truth who comes from the Father, he will testify on my behalf. You also are to testify because you have been with me from the beginning.

"I still have many things to say to you, but you cannot bear them now. When the Spirit of truth comes, he will guide you into all the truth; for he will not speak on his own, but will speak whatever he hears, and he will declare to you the things that are to come. He will glorify me, because he will take what is mine and declare it to you.

"All that the Father has is mine. For this reason I said that he will take what is mine and declare it to you."

The Gospel of the Lord. **Praise to you, Lord Jesus Christ.**

Pentecost is the Greek word for the Jewish festival that takes place on the fiftieth day after Passover. Fifty days after Jesus' resurrection, the Holy Spirit descended upon Mary and the apostles. For Christians, Pentecost is the feast of the coming of the Holy Spirit.

Saint Luke describes the coming of the Holy Spirit like fire — full of energy and power, dazzling everyone around.

People from all over the world are amazed at the apostles' message. Saint Luke underlines the fact that Jesus came for all humankind — for Jews, converts (Jews not born Jewish) and people from every conceivable country on earth.

God's deeds of power are so great that they cannot be counted, but the greatest of these is that he sent his Son to save us. The disciples proclaimed God's marvellous deed — the death and resurrection of Jesus.

The Advocate is another name for the Holy Spirit, sent by Jesus to be our helper and guide until the end of time. An advocate is someone who speaks on another's behalf, often to make their case for them. Jesus promises that the Holy Spirit will be our advocate.

Solemnity of the Most Holy Trinity

Moses spoke to the people saying, "Ask now about former ages, long before your own, ever since the day that God created man on the earth; ask from one end of heaven to the other: 'Has anything so great as this ever happened or has its like ever been heard of?'

"Has any people ever heard the voice of a god speaking out of a fire, as you have heard, and lived? Or has any god ever attempted to go and take a nation for himself from the midst of another nation, by trials, by signs and wonders, by war, by a mighty hand and an outstretched arm, and by terrifying displays of power, as the Lord your God did for you in Egypt before your very eyes?

"So acknowledge today and take to heart that the Lord is God in heaven above and on the earth beneath; there is no other. Keep his statutes and his commandments, which I am commanding you today for your own well-being and that of your descendants after you, so that you may long remain in the land that the Lord your God is giving you for all time."

The word of the Lord. **Thanks be to God.**

Psalm 33

R. **Blessed the people the Lord has chosen as his heritage.**

The word of the Lord is upright,
and all his work is done in faithfulness.
He loves righteousness and justice;
the earth is full of the steadfast love of the Lord. R.

By the word of the Lord the heavens were made,
and all their host by the breath of his mouth.
For he spoke, and it came to be;
he commanded, and it stood firm. R.

Truly the eye of the Lord is on those who fear him,
on those who hope in his steadfast love,
to deliver their souls from death,
and to keep them alive in famine. R.

Our soul waits for the Lord;
he is our help and shield.
Let your steadfast love, O Lord, be upon us,
even as we hope in you. R.

A reading from the Letter of Saint Paul to the Romans (8.14-17)

Brothers and sisters: All who are led by the Spirit of God are sons and daughters of God. For you did not receive a spirit of slavery to fall back into fear, but you have received a spirit of adoption to sonship. When we cry, "Abba! Father!" it is that very Spirit bearing witness with our spirit that we are children of God, and if children, then heirs, heirs of God and joint heirs with Christ — if in fact, we suffer with him so that we may also be glorified with him.

The word of the Lord. **Thanks be to God.**

A reading from the holy Gospel according to Matthew (28.16-20)

The eleven disciples went to Galilee, to the mountain to which Jesus had directed them. When they saw him, they worshipped him; but some doubted.

And Jesus came and said to them, "All authority in heaven and on earth has been given to me. Go therefore and make disciples of all nations, baptizing them in the name of the Father and of the Son and of the Holy Spirit, and teaching them to obey everything that I have commanded you.

"And remember, I am with you always, to the end of the age."

The Gospel of the Lord. **Praise to you, Lord Jesus Christ.**

The Trinity is three persons in one God: the Father, the Son and the Holy Spirit. Today, on Trinity Sunday, we celebrate this mystery.

Deuteronomy is the fifth book in the Hebrew Scriptures or Old Testament. It is a Greek word meaning 'the second law,' or the second time God gave his people his law. It tells us that God is one and so the people of God must be united.

God freed the people of Israel, who were slaves in Egypt (see the map, page 320). This important event shows how God keeps his promise to take care of his people.

Children of God describes all of us: God our Father loves us and takes care of us.

We are heirs of God because we are God's children and children inherit from their parents. All God's riches are ours — not only the things he has created, but also his life, which we share.

Galilee is a province in the north of Palestine (see the map, page 320). Nazareth, the town where Jesus lived with his parents, is in Galilee. So is the Sea of Galilee, where some of Jesus' disciples worked as fishermen. Jesus spent a lot of time preaching in this area. In Jerusalem, to the south, Jesus was known as a Galilean, because of his northern accent.

"I am with you always" is the promise Jesus made when he appeared after his resurrection. Jesus is with us when we gather in his name as a community, when we listen to God's word, when we celebrate the eucharist, and when we share his love with others.

Solemnity of the Most Holy Body and Blood of Christ

Moses came and told the people all the words of the Lord and all the ordinances; and all the people answered with one voice, and said, "All the words that the Lord has spoken we will do."

And Moses wrote down all the words of the Lord. He rose early in the morning, and built an altar at the foot of the mountain, and set up twelve pillars, corresponding to the twelve tribes of Israel. He sent young men of the children of Israel, who offered burnt offerings and sacrificed oxen as offerings of well-being to the Lord. Moses took half of the blood and put it in basins, and half of the blood he dashed against the altar.

Then he took the book of the covenant, and read it in the hearing of the people; and they said, "All that the Lord has spoken we will do, and we will be obedient."

Moses took the blood and dashed it on the people, and said, "See the blood of the covenant that the Lord has made with you in accordance with all these words."

The word of the Lord. **Thanks be to God.**

Psalm 116

R. I will lift up the cup of salvation,
and call on the name of the Lord.

or Alleluia!

What shall I return to the Lord
for all his bounty to me?
I will lift up the cup of salvation
and call on the name of the Lord. R.

Precious in the sight of the Lord
is the death of his faithful ones.
O Lord, I am your servant, the son of your serving girl.
You have loosed my bonds. R.

I will offer to you a thanksgiving sacrifice
and call on the name of the Lord.
I will pay my vows to the Lord
in the presence of all his people. R.

A reading from the Letter to the Hebrews (9.11-15)

Brothers and sisters: When Christ came as a high priest of the good things that have come, then through the greater and perfect tent — not made with hands, that is, not of this creation — he entered once for all into the Holy Place, not with the blood of goats and calves, but with his own blood, thus obtaining eternal redemption.

For if the blood of goats and bulls, with the sprinkling of the ashes of a heifer, sanctifies those who have been defiled so that their flesh is purified, how much more will the blood of Christ, who through the eternal Spirit offered himself without blemish to God, purify our conscience from dead works to worship the living God!

For this reason Christ is the mediator of a new covenant, so that those who are called may receive the promised eternal inheritance, because a death has occurred that redeems them from the transgressions under the first covenant.

The word of the Lord. **Thanks be to God.**

A reading from the holy Gospel according to Mark (14.12-16, 22-26)

On the first day of Unleavened Bread, when the Passover lamb is sacrificed, the disciples said to Jesus, "Where do you want us to go and make the preparations for you to eat the Passover?"

So he sent two of his disciples, saying to them, "Go into the city, and a man carrying a jar of water will meet you; follow him, and wherever he enters, say to the owner of the house, 'The Teacher asks, "Where is my guest room where I may eat the Passover with my disciples?"' He will show you a large room upstairs, furnished and ready. Make preparations for us there."

So the disciples set out and went to the city, and found everything as he had told them; and they prepared the Passover meal.

While they were eating, he took a loaf of bread, and after blessing it he broke it, gave it to them, and said, "Take; this is my Body."

Then he took a cup, and after giving thanks he gave it to them, and all of them drank from it. He said to them, "This is my Blood of the covenant, which is poured out for many. Truly I tell you, I will never again drink of the fruit of the vine until that day when I drink it new in the kingdom of God."

When they had sung the hymn, they went out to the Mount of Olives.

The Gospel of the Lord. **Praise to you, Lord Jesus Christ.**

The twelve tribes of Israel were the descendants of the twelve sons of Jacob, who was also called Israel. The Bible often uses this term to refer to the whole Jewish people.

Oxen were strong, valuable animals: they pulled the plough to prepare the land for seeding and then pulled the wagons to bring in the crops at harvest time. Sacrificing (killing) an ox meant giving up something important.

Being obedient means doing what God asks. When the people of Israel say, "We will be obedient," they are promising to do God's will for the rest of their lives.

A vow is a solemn promise to be faithful. When a man and a woman marry, they vow to love God and one another. Priests, religious brothers and sisters vow to be faithful to God. Vows are 'paid' when people keep their promises.

A mediator brings together two people who don't know each other or who cannot agree. Christ is our mediator; he acts as a link between human beings and God, and helps us dialogue with one another.

For Passover, or the festival of Unleavened Bread, each Jewish family prepares a Passover lamb. At the festival dinner, they gather to recall how God freed their ancestors from slavery in Egypt. This follows the instructions that the Angel of God gave to the Israelites, to sacrifice a spring lamb as they prepared to flee Egypt.

The Mount of Olives is a hillside near Jerusalem on which olive trees grow. Jesus often went there to pray and rest after he had been teaching. The Garden of Gethsemane is at the base of the Mount of Olives, and Jesus was praying there when the soldiers came to arrest him.

11th Sunday in Ordinary Time

Thus says the Lord God:

"I myself will take a sprig
from the lofty top of a cedar;
I will set it out.
I will break off a tender one
from the topmost of its young twigs;
I myself will plant it
on a high and lofty mountain.

"On the mountain height of Israel
I will plant it,
in order that it may produce boughs and bear fruit,
and become a noble cedar.
Under it every kind of bird will live;
in the shade of its branches will nest
winged creatures of every kind.

"All the trees of the field shall know
that I am the Lord.
I bring low the high tree,
I make high the low tree;
I dry up the green tree
and make the dry tree flourish.
I the Lord have spoken;
I will accomplish it."

The word of the Lord. **Thanks be to God.**

R. **Lord, it is good to give thanks to you.**

It is good to give thanks to the Lord,
to sing praises to your name, O Most High;
to declare your steadfast love in the morning,
and your faithfulness by night. R.

The righteous flourish like the palm tree,
and grow like a cedar in Lebanon.
They are planted in the house of the Lord;
they flourish in the courts of our God. R.

In old age they still produce fruit;
they are always green and full of sap,
showing that the Lord is upright;
he is my rock, and there is no unrighteousness in him. R.

A reading from the second Letter of Saint Paul to the Corinthians (5.6-10)

Brothers and sisters, we are always confident, even though we know that while we are at home in the body we are away from the Lord — for we walk by faith, not by sight. Yes, we do have confidence, and we would rather be away from the body and at home with the Lord.

So whether we are at home or away, we make it our aim to please him. For all of us must appear before the judgment seat of Christ, so that each may receive recompense for what he or she has done in the body, whether good or evil.

The word of the Lord. **Thanks be to God.**

Such a large crowd gathered around Jesus that he got into a boat and began to teach them using many parables.

Jesus said: "The kingdom of God is as if a man would scatter seed on the ground, and would sleep and rise night and day, and the seed would sprout and grow, without his knowing how. The earth produces of itself, first the stalk, then the head, then the full grain in the head. But when the grain is ripe, at once he goes in with the sickle, because the harvest has come."

Jesus also said, "With what can we compare the kingdom of God, or what parable will we use for it? It is like a mustard seed, which, when sown upon the ground, is the smallest of all the seeds on earth; yet when it is sown it grows up and becomes the greatest of all shrubs, and puts forth large branches, so that the birds of the air can make nests in its shade."

With many such parables Jesus spoke the word to them, as they were able to hear it; he did not speak to them except in parables, but he explained everything in private to his disciples.

The Gospel of the Lord. **Praise to you, Lord Jesus Christ.**

When the Bible wants to show God's power, it often says that God has spoken. In the creation story, for example, God says "Let there be light" and there is light. God speaks the word, and it is so. Ezekiel likens the people of God to a forest that is growing and spreading; God says the word, and the trees either flourish or die.

The cedar in Lebanon is an ancient tree that can be seen on the flag of Lebanon today. These trees are famous for their size and hardiness; there are some trees today that stand 35 metres tall and have trunks 12 metres around. At the time today's psalm was written, it was a great compliment to be compared to a cedar of Lebanon.

Saint Paul reminds us that while we are at home in the body — while we enjoy the gift of life that God gives us — our true home is with God. We must never forget to avoid sin and follow God's laws while we live in the body.

When Jesus was teaching the crowds, sometimes there were so many people that he couldn't be seen or heard. In today's Gospel, Jesus gets into a boat instead. This way, everyone could gather on the shore in order to see and hear Jesus as he spoke to them from the boat.

A sickle is a crescent-shaped hand tool that is used to cut the stalks of grains and grasses. It is a good sign in today's parable that the man is using his sickle, because this means his crop is ready to be harvested.

Listen to me, O coastlands,
pay attention, you peoples from far away!
The Lord called me before I was born,
while I was in my mother's womb he named me.

He made my mouth like a sharp sword,
in the shadow of his hand he hid me;
he made me a polished arrow,
in his quiver he hid me away.

And the Lord said to me,
"You are my servant, Israel, in whom I will be glorified."
But I said, "I have laboured in vain,
I have spent my strength for nothing and vanity;
yet surely my cause is with the Lord,
and my reward with my God."

And now the Lord says,
who formed me in the womb to be his servant,
to bring Jacob back to him,
and that Israel might be gathered to him,
for I am honoured in the sight of the Lord,
and my God has become my strength.

He says,
"It is too small a thing that you should be my servant
to raise up the tribes of Jacob
and to restore the survivors of Israel;
I will give you as a light to the nations,
that my salvation may reach to the end of the earth."

The word of the Lord. **Thanks be to God.**

R. **I praise you, for I am wonderfully made.**

O Lord, you have searched me and known me.
You know when I sit down and when I rise up;
you discern my thoughts from far away.
You search out my path and my lying down,
and are acquainted with all my ways. R.

For it was you who formed my inward parts;
you knit me together in my mother's womb.
I praise you,
for I am fearfully and wonderfully made. R.

Wonderful are your works; that I know very well.
My frame was not hidden from you,
when I was being made in secret,
intricately woven in the depths of the earth. R.

A reading from the Acts of the Apostles (13.22-26)

In those days, Paul said: "God made David king of our ancestors. In his testimony about him God said, 'I have found David, son of Jesse, to be a man after my heart, who will carry out all my wishes.'

"Of this man's posterity God has brought to Israel a Saviour, Jesus, as he promised; before his coming John had already proclaimed a baptism of repentance to all the people of Israel. And as John was finishing his work, he said, 'What do you suppose that I am? I am not he. No, but one is coming after me; I am not worthy to untie the thong of the sandals on his feet.'

"You descendants of Abraham's family, and others who fear God, to us the message of this salvation has been sent."

The word of the Lord. **Thanks be to God.**

The time came for Elizabeth to give birth, and she bore a son. Her neighbours and relatives heard that the Lord had shown his great mercy to her, and they rejoiced with her.

On the eighth day they came to circumcise the child, and they were going to name him Zechariah after his father. But his mother said, "No; he is to be called John." They said to her, "None of your relatives has this name." Then they began motioning to his father to find out what name he wanted to give him.

He asked for a writing tablet and wrote, "His name is John." And all of them were amazed. Immediately his mouth was opened and his tongue freed, and he began to speak, praising God.

Fear came over all their neighbours, and all these things were talked about throughout the entire hill country of Judea. All who heard them pondered them and said, "What then will this child become?" For, indeed, the hand of the Lord was with him.

The child grew and became strong in spirit, and he was in the wilderness until the day he appeared publicly to Israel.

The Gospel of the Lord. **Praise to you, Lord Jesus Christ.**

The womb is that part of the woman's body where a baby grows until it is time to be born. When we name something, we recognize that we have a connection to it; the message in today's reading from Isaiah is that God names us — God knows about us and cares for us — even before we are born.

A quiver is a bag that holds arrows for a warrior or hunter so that they will not be lost or bent. Arrows are valuable and must be cared for, so that they will be ready for use when needed.

Someone's posterity is their sons and daughters and their descendants. Jesus was part of King David's posterity, as we see in the opening genealogy in Saint Matthew's Gospel.

John the Baptist carried out a ministry of baptism of repentance, asking people to turn away from sin and follow God's laws. To become followers of Jesus, we must be sorry for our sins and follow God's law of love.

To untie the thong of the sandals of someone was usually the task of a slave. If a person is unworthy to carry out this lowly task, their social standing must be far below that of a slave.

When people heard about the unusual way John the Baptist received his name, they knew he was going to be someone special. One way of expressing this is to say that the hand of the Lord was with him — John enjoyed the favour of the Lord.

13th Sunday in Ordinary Time

God did not make death, and he does not delight in the death of the living. For he created all things so that they might exist; the generative forces of the world are wholesome, and there is no destructive poison in them, and the dominion of Hades is not on earth. For righteousness is immortal.

For God created man for incorruption, and made him in the image of his own eternity, but through the devil's envy death entered the world, and those who belong to his company experience it.

The word of the Lord. **Thanks be to God.**

Psalm 30

R. **I will extol you, Lord, for you have raised me up.**

I will extol you, O Lord, for you have drawn me up,
and did not let my foes rejoice over me.
O Lord, you brought up my soul from Sheol,
restored me to life from among those gone down to the Pit. R.

Sing praises to the Lord, O you his faithful ones,
and give thanks to his holy name.
For his anger is but for a moment;
his favour is for a lifetime.
Weeping may linger for the night,
but joy comes with the morning. R.

Hear, O Lord, and be gracious to me!
O Lord, be my helper!
You have turned my mourning into dancing.
O Lord my God, I will give thanks to you forever. R.

Brothers and sisters: Now as you excel in everything — in faith, in speech, in knowledge, in utmost eagerness, and in our love for you — so we want you to excel also in this generous undertaking.

For you know the generous act of our Lord Jesus Christ, that though he was rich, yet for your sakes he became poor so that by his poverty you might become rich.

I do not mean that there should be relief for others and pressure on you, but it is a question of a fair balance between your present abundance and their need, so that their abundance may be for your need, in order that there may be a fair balance.

As it is written, "The one who had much did not have too much, and the one who had little did not have too little."

The word of the Lord. **Thanks be to God.**

For the shorter version, omit the indented parts.

When Jesus had crossed in the boat to the other side, a great crowd gathered around him; and he was by the sea. Then one of the synagogue leaders named Jairus came and, when he saw Jesus, fell at his feet and begged him repeatedly, "My little daughter is at the point of death. Come and lay your hands on her, so that she may be made well, and live." So Jesus went with him. And a large crowd followed him.

> and pressed in on him. Now there was a woman who had been suffering from hemorrhages for twelve years. She had endured much under many physicians, and had spent all that she had; and she was no better, but rather grew worse. She had heard about Jesus, and came up behind him in the crowd and touched his cloak, for she said, "If I but touch his clothes, I will be made well." Immediately her hemorrhage stopped; and she felt in her body that she was healed of her disease.
>
> Immediately aware that power had gone forth from him, Jesus turned about in the crowd and said, "Who touched my

191

clothes?" And his disciples said to him, "You see the crowd pressing in on you; how can you say, 'Who touched me'?"

He looked all around to see who had done it. But the woman, knowing what had happened to her, came in fear and trembling, fell down before him, and told him the whole truth. Jesus said to her, "Daughter, your faith has made you well; go in peace, and be healed of your disease."

While Jesus was still speaking,

Some people came from the leader's house to say, "Your daughter is dead. Why trouble the teacher any further?" But overhearing what they said, Jesus said to the leader of the synagogue, "Do not fear, only believe."

Jesus allowed no one to follow him. When they came to the house of the leader of the synagogue, he saw a commotion, people weeping and wailing loudly. When he had entered, he said to them, "Why do you make a commotion and weep? The child is not dead but sleeping." And they laughed at him.

Then Jesus put them all outside, and took the child's father and mother and those who were with him, and went in where the child was. He took her by the hand and said to her, "Talitha cum," which means, "Little girl, get up!" And immediately the girl got up and began to walk about for she was twelve years of age.

At this they were overcome with amazement. He strictly ordered them that no one should know this, and told them to give her something to eat.

The Gospel of the Lord.
Praise to you, Lord Jesus Christ.

KEY WORDS

Hades is a Greek word for the underworld, which we sometimes call Hell. It is a place of death. The book of Wisdom tells us that death and destruction do not control our world. God created the world and knows that it is good.

Eternity means time without beginning or end: a past, present and future that always exist. God is eternal because there is no limit to his existence. God created us to share his life in infinite time, rejoicing in eternity.

Sheol is a Hebrew word for the underworld. The Israelites believed that when people died, their soul went down into Sheol, which was described as a pit. It was a silent place, where people could no longer worship God. The psalmist is happy because God's saving power has drawn him up out of this pit.

Many people are fortunate to live with abundance, more than they need; others are not so lucky, and have very little upon which to live. Saint Paul teaches us to share with others from our abundance, so that everyone can have enough to live on.

Talitha cum is Aramaic for "Little girl, get up!" While the Gospels of Matthew and Luke also include this miracle, only Mark gives us the Aramaic words that Jesus spoke. This gives the account a special flavour and helps us feel closer in time to Jesus.

July 8

14th Sunday in Ordinary Time

A spirit entered into me and set me on my feet;
and I heard one speaking to me:
"Son of man, I am sending you to the children of Israel,
to a nation of rebels who have rebelled against me;
they and their ancestors have transgressed against me to this very day.
The descendants are impudent and stubborn.
I am sending you to them, and you shall say to them,
'Thus says the Lord God.'
Whether they hear or refuse to hear
(for they are a rebellious house),
they shall know that there has been a Prophet among them."

The word of the Lord. **Thanks be to God.**

Psalm 123

R̰ **Our eyes look to the Lord, until he has mercy upon us.**

To you I lift up my eyes —
O you who are enthroned in the heavens —
as the eyes of servants
look to the hand of their master. R̰

As the eyes of a maid
to the hand of her mistress,
so our eyes look to the Lord our God,
until he has mercy upon us. R̰

Have mercy upon us, O Lord, have mercy,
for we have had more than enough of contempt.
Our soul has had more than its fill of the scorn
of those who are at ease, of the contempt of the proud. R̰

A reading from the second Letter of Saint Paul to the Corinthians (12.7-10)

Brothers and sisters: Considering the exceptional character of the revelations, to keep me from being too elated, a thorn was given me in the flesh, a messenger of Satan to torment me, to keep me from being too elated.

Three times I appealed to the Lord about this, that it would leave me, but he said to me, "My grace is sufficient for you, for power is made perfect in weakness."

So, I will boast all the more gladly of my weaknesses, so that the power of Christ may dwell in me. Therefore I am content with weaknesses, insults, hardships, persecutions, and calamities for the sake of Christ; for whenever I am weak, then I am strong.

The word of the Lord. **Thanks be to God.**

A reading from the holy Gospel according to Mark (6.1-6)

Jesus came to his hometown, and his disciples followed him. On the Sabbath he began to teach in the synagogue, and many who heard him were astounded. They said, "Where did this man get all this? What is this wisdom that has been given to him? What deeds of power are being done by his hands! Is not this the carpenter, the son of Mary and brother of James and Joses and Judas and Simon, and are not his sisters here with us?" And they took offence at him.

Then Jesus said to them, "A Prophet is not without honour, except in his hometown, and among his own kin, and in his own house."

And Jesus could do no deed of power there, except that he laid his hands on a few sick people and cured them. And Jesus was amazed at their unbelief.

Then he went about among the villages teaching.

The Gospel of the Lord. **Praise to you, Lord Jesus Christ.**

Ezekiel was one of the most important prophets in Israel. He lived during a time when many of the people of Jerusalem were taken prisoner and forced to live far away in Babylon. The king and Ezekiel were taken away, too. Ezekiel helped the people follow God's ways far from home.

The people of Israel had turned away from God and were impudent and stubborn (not showing God proper respect and refusing to change). God chose Ezekiel as a prophet to bring the people back to God. We all need to be willing to change our hearts if we love God.

Saint Paul endured hardship and imprisonment for the sake of the Gospel, but he didn't complain of his sufferings. Instead, he says he can boast of his weaknesses because they make him rely on God who gives him everything. Saint Paul is thankful for all God's gifts and finds strength in the grace of God.

The synagogue is a place where Jews gather to read the Scriptures and pray. Sometimes it is called a temple.

A deed of power is an extraordinary event that cannot be explained except by the grace and power of God. Jesus performed many miracles to show that he was sent by God, and to let people know that God cares about those who suffer. When Jesus performed a miracle, it was always so that people's faith could grow.

197

15th Sunday in Ordinary Time

Amaziah, the priest of Bethel, said to Amos, "O seer, go, flee away to the land of Judah, earn your bread there, and prophesy there; but never again prophesy at Bethel, for it is the king's sanctuary, and it is a temple of the kingdom."

Then Amos answered Amaziah, "I am no Prophet, nor a Prophet's son; but I am a herdsman, and a dresser of sycamore trees, and the Lord took me from following the flock, and the Lord said to me, 'Go, prophesy to my people Israel.'"

The word of the Lord. **Thanks be to God.**

Psalm 85

R. **Show us your steadfast love, O Lord,
and grant us your salvation.**

Let me hear what God the Lord will speak,
for he will speak peace to his people.
Surely his salvation is at hand for those who fear him,
that his glory may dwell in our land. R.

Steadfast love and faithfulness will meet;
righteousness and peace will kiss each other.
Faithfulness will spring up from the ground,
and righteousness will look down from the sky. R.

The Lord will give what is good,
and our land will yield its increase.
Righteousness will go before him,
and will make a path for his steps. R.

A reading from the Letter of Saint Paul to the Ephesians (1.3-14)

The shorter version ends at the asterisks.

Blessed be the God and Father of our Lord Jesus Christ, who has blessed us in Christ with every spiritual blessing in the heavenly places, just as he chose us in Christ before the foundation of the world to be holy and blameless before him in love.

He destined us for adoption to sonship as his own through Jesus Christ, according to the good pleasure of his will, to the praise of his glorious grace that he freely bestowed on us in the Beloved.

In Christ we have redemption through his blood, the forgiveness of our trespasses, according to the riches of his grace that he lavished on us.

With all wisdom and insight God has made known to us the mystery of his will, according to his good pleasure that he set forth in Christ, as a plan for the fullness of time, to gather up all things in Christ, things in heaven and things on earth.

* * *

In Christ we have also obtained an inheritance, having been destined according to the purpose of him who accomplishes all things according to his counsel and will, so that we, who were the first to set our hope on Christ, might live for the praise of his glory.

In him you also, when you had heard the word of truth, the Gospel of your salvation, and had believed in him, were marked with the seal of the promised Holy Spirit.

This is the pledge of our inheritance toward redemption as God's own people, to the praise of his glory.

The word of the Lord. **Thanks be to God.**

Jesus called the twelve and began to send them out two by two, and gave them authority over the unclean spirits. He ordered them to take nothing for their journey except a staff; no bread, no bag, no money in their belts; but to wear sandals and not to put on two tunics.

Jesus said to them, "Wherever you enter a house, stay there until you leave the place. If any place will not welcome you and they refuse to hear you, as you leave, shake off the dust that is on your feet as a testimony against them."

So the twelve went out and proclaimed that all should repent. They cast out many demons, and anointed with oil many who were sick and cured them.

The Gospel of the Lord. **Praise to you, Lord Jesus Christ.**

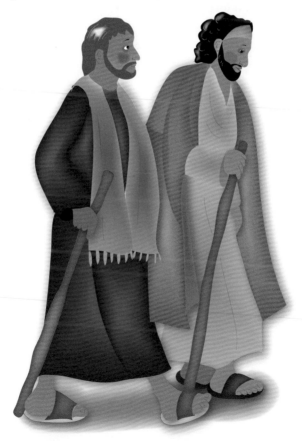

Amos was a prophet, a friend of God. He lived about 800 years before Jesus. Some people he met were rich because they made the poor work hard for them and paid them very little. Amos taught these rich people that they must treat others fairly and help the poor.

Amos is a good example of how a Prophet speaks for God. His message reminds people that they need to focus on God and love everyone they meet. Prophets do not choose to be God's messengers: God chooses them for this important job.

Saying "Blessed be God" is a way of praising God. We are saying, 'Let the whole world know how great and wonderful God is!'

Redemption is another word for setting someone free. Long ago, slaves could be set free if someone bought, or redeemed, them. God redeems us so that we are no longer slaves to anything or anyone.

In the past, many people believed that anyone who acted strangely was evil or had unclean spirits. Jesus showed that he had the power to heal both body and spirit, and he shared this power with the apostles.

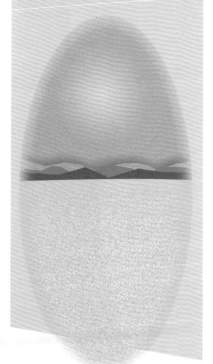

16th Sunday in Ordinary Time

"Woe to the shepherds who destroy and scatter the sheep of my pasture!" says the Lord. Therefore, thus says the Lord, the God of Israel, concerning the shepherds who shepherd my people: It is you who have scattered my flock, and have driven them away, and you have not attended to them.

"So I will attend to you for your evil doings," says the Lord. "Then I myself will gather the remnant of my flock out of all the lands where I have driven them, and I will bring them back to their fold, and they shall be fruitful and multiply. I will raise up shepherds over them who will shepherd them, and they shall not fear any longer, or be dismayed, nor shall any be missing," says the Lord.

"The days are surely coming," says the Lord, "when I will raise up for David a righteous Branch, and he shall reign as king and deal wisely, and shall execute justice and righteousness in the land. In his days Judah will be saved and Israel will live in safety. And this is the name by which he will be called: 'The Lord is our righteousness.'"

The word of the Lord. **Thanks be to God.**

Psalm 23

R. **The Lord is my shepherd; I shall not want.**

The Lord is my shepherd, I shall not want.
He makes me lie down in green pastures;
he leads me beside still waters;
he restores my soul. R.

He leads me in right paths for his name's sake.
Even though I walk through the darkest valley, I fear no evil;
for you are with me;
your rod and your staff — they comfort me. R.

You prepare a table before me
in the presence of my enemies;
you anoint my head with oil;
my cup overflows. R.

Surely goodness and mercy shall follow me
all the days of my life,
and I shall dwell in the house of the Lord
my whole life long. R.

A reading from the Letter of Saint Paul to the Ephesians (2.13-18)

Brothers and sisters: Now in Christ Jesus you who once were far off have been brought near by the blood of Christ. For he is our peace; in his flesh he has made both Jews and Gentiles into one and has broken down the dividing wall, that is, the hostility between us.

He has abolished the law with its commandments and ordinances, that he might create in himself one New Man in place of the two, thus making peace, and might reconcile both groups to God in one body through the Cross, thus putting to death that hostility through it.

So Christ Jesus came and proclaimed peace to you who were far off and peace to those who were near; for through him both of us have access in one Spirit to the Father.

The word of the Lord. **Thanks be to God.**

A reading from the holy Gospel according to Mark (6.30-34)

The Apostles returned from their mission. They gathered around Jesus, and told him all that they had done and taught.

He said to them, "Come away to a deserted place all by yourselves and rest a while." For many were coming and going, and they had no leisure even to eat. And they went away in the boat to a deserted place by themselves.

Now many saw them going and recognized them, and they hurried there on foot from all the towns and arrived ahead of them. As Jesus went ashore, he saw a great crowd; and he had compassion for them, because they were like sheep without a shepherd; and he began to teach them many things.

The Gospel of the Lord. **Praise to you, Lord Jesus Christ.**

Good shepherds take care of their sheep and keep them safe day and night. Jeremiah is angry at the bad shepherds or leaders of Israel who have led the people away from God. Today we call a church leader a pastor, a word that literally means "shepherd."

A Branch for David refers to the descendants of David: his children and all who will be born from them. When Jeremiah announces that God will raise up a new branch, he is foretelling the birth of Jesus, who will be born of the House of David.

To execute justice is to make sure that God's law of love is observed all the time. This is the only way people can live in peace and joy. By calling us to love one another as God has loved us, Jesus shows us how to do this.

Saint Paul is known as the Apostle to the Gentiles (non-Jewish people). Before the time of Jesus, the Jewish people understood God to be the God of Israel only. But in Saint Paul's letters and in the Acts of the Apostles, we see how the disciples in the early Church came to understand that all people — Jews and Gentiles alike — are made one in the blood of Christ. This was a difficult and radical new teaching.

17th Sunday in Ordinary Time

A reading from the second book of Kings (4.42-44)

A man came bringing food from the first fruits to Elisha, the man of God: twenty loaves of barley and fresh ears of grain in his sack. Elisha said, "Give it to the people and let them eat."

But his servant said, "How can I set this before a hundred people?" So Elisha repeated, "Give it to the people and let them eat, for thus says the Lord, 'They shall eat and have some left.'"

The servant set it before them, they ate, and had some left, according to the word of the Lord.

The word of the Lord. **Thanks be to God.**

Psalm 145

R. **You open your hand to feed us, Lord; you satisfy all our needs.**

All your works shall give thanks to you, O Lord,
and all your faithful shall bless you.
They shall speak of the glory of your kingdom,
and tell of your power. R.

The eyes of all look to you,
and you give them their food in due season.
You open your hand,
satisfying the desire of every living thing. R.

The Lord is just in all his ways,
and kind in all his doings.
The Lord is near to all who call on him,
to all who call on him in truth. R.

A reading from the Letter of Saint Paul to the Ephesians (4.1-6)

Brothers and sisters: I, the prisoner in the Lord, beg you to lead a life worthy of the calling to which you have been called, with all humility and gentleness, with patience, bearing with one another in love, making every effort to maintain the unity of the Spirit in the bond of peace.

There is one body and one Spirit, just as you were called to the one hope of your calling, one Lord, one faith, one baptism, one God and Father of all, who is above all and through all and in all.

The word of the Lord. **Thanks be to God.**

A reading from the holy Gospel according to John (6.1-15)

Jesus went to the other side of the Sea of Galilee, also called the Sea of Tiberias. A large crowd kept following him, because they saw the signs that he was doing for the sick. Jesus went up the mountain and sat down there with his disciples. Now the Passover, the festival of the Jews, was near.

When he looked up and saw a large crowd coming toward him, Jesus said to Philip, "Where are we to buy bread for these people to eat?" He said this to test him, for he himself knew what he was going to do. Philip answered him, "Six months' wages would not buy enough bread for each of them to get a little."

One of his disciples, Andrew, Simon Peter's brother, said to Jesus, "There is a boy here who has five barley loaves and two fish. But what are they among so many people?" Jesus said, "Make the people sit down." Now there was a great deal of grass in the place; so they sat down, about five thousand in all.

Then Jesus took the loaves, and when he had given thanks, he distributed them to those who were seated; so also the fish, as much as they wanted. When they were satisfied, he told his disciples, "Gather up the fragments left over, so that nothing may be lost." So they gathered them up, and from the fragments of the five barley loaves, left by those who had eaten, they filled twelve baskets.

When the people saw the sign that he had done, they began to say, "This is indeed the Prophet who is to come into the world." When Jesus realized that they were about to come and take him by force to make him king, he withdrew again to the mountain by himself.

The Gospel of the Lord. **Praise to you, Lord Jesus Christ.**

In the Bible, the two books of Kings tell the story of a time when Israel was ruled by kings. They begin with the death of King David, nearly 1,000 years before Jesus was born, and end when the Babylonians capture Jerusalem, nearly 600 years before Jesus. The writer wants us to see how God helps his people throughout history.

Toward the end of Elijah's life, God told Elijah to anoint Elisha to be prophet after him, to guide the people so they would not stray from God. Elisha lived about 850 years before Jesus, and was a prophet in Israel for sixty years.

Humility means helping or serving others without expecting any reward or praise. Jesus shows true humility in his readiness to heal the sick and feed the hungry, and we are called to follow his example.

A bond is a tie to someone we care about. In his letter to the Ephesians, Saint Paul helps us to see that building a bond of peace, a link of caring, among ourselves is one of the best ways to maintain unity.

There are many different Christian churches today. Because Jesus is our one Lord, Christians are always working to become one community of faith. We do this by getting to know each other and praying together, nurturing the faith that Jesus taught us.

Although the word mountain is used in today's Gospel, in Israel there are no high mountains. Rather, when the Gospel speaks of a 'mountain,' we can imagine a hill. Jesus often went up into the hills to pray and to speak to the people who followed him.

18th Sunday in Ordinary Time

The whole congregation of the children of Israel complained against Moses and Aaron in the wilderness. The children of Israel said to them, "If only we had died by the hand of the Lord in the land of Egypt, when we sat by the fleshpots and ate our fill of bread; for you have brought us out into this wilderness to kill this whole assembly with hunger."

Then the Lord said to Moses, "I am going to rain bread from heaven for you, and each day the people shall go out and gather enough for that day. In that way I will test them, whether they will follow my instruction or not.

"I have heard the complaining of the children of Israel; say to them, 'At twilight you shall eat meat, and in the morning you shall have your fill of bread; then you shall know that I am the Lord your God.'"

In the evening quails came up and covered the camp; and in the morning there was a layer of dew around the camp. When the layer of dew lifted, there on the surface of the wilderness was a fine flaky substance, as fine as frost on the ground.

When the children of Israel saw it, they said to one another, "What is it?" For they did not know what it was. Moses said to them, "It is the bread that the Lord has given you to eat."

The house of Israel called it manna.

The word of the Lord. **Thanks be to God.**

R̶ **The Lord gave them the bread of heaven.**

Things that we have heard and known,
that our ancestors have told us, we will not hide;
we will tell to the coming generation
the glorious deeds of the Lord, and his might.
and the wonders that he has done. R̶

He commanded the skies above,
and opened the doors of heaven;
he rained down on them manna to eat,
and gave them the bread of heaven. R̶

Man ate of the bread of Angels;
he sent them food in abundance.
And he brought them to his holy hill,
to the mountain that his right hand had won. R̶

A reading from the Letter of Saint Paul to the Ephesians (4.17, 20-24)

Brothers and sisters: Now this I affirm and insist on in the Lord: you must no longer live as the Gentiles live, in the futility of their minds.

That is not the way you learned Christ! For surely you have heard about him and were taught in him, as truth is in Jesus.

You were taught to put away your former way of life, your old self, corrupt and deluded by its lusts, and to be renewed in the spirit of your minds, and to clothe yourselves with the New Man, created according to the likeness of God in true righteousness and holiness.

The word of the Lord. **Thanks be to God.**

When the crowd saw that neither Jesus nor his disciples were at the place where Jesus had given the bread, they themselves got into the boats and went to Capernaum looking for Jesus.

When they found him on the other side of the sea, they said to him, "Rabbi, when did you come here?" Jesus answered them, "Very truly, I tell you, you are looking for me, not because you saw signs, but because you ate your fill of the loaves. Do not work for the food that perishes, but for the food that endures for eternal life, which the Son of Man will give you. For it is on him that God the Father has set his seal."

Then they said to Jesus, "What must we do to perform the works of God?" Jesus answered them, "This is the work of God, that you believe in him whom he has sent." So they said to him, "What sign are you going to give us then, so that we may see it and believe you? What work are you performing? Our ancestors ate the manna in the wilderness; as it is written, 'He gave them bread from heaven to eat.'"

Then Jesus said to them, "Very truly, I tell you, it was not Moses who gave you the bread from heaven, but it is my Father who gives you the true bread from heaven. For the bread of God is that which comes down from heaven and gives life to the world."

They said to him, "Sir, give us this bread always." Jesus said to them, "I am the bread of life. Whoever comes to me will never be hungry, and whoever believes in me will never be thirsty."

The Gospel of the Lord.
**Praise to you,
Lord Jesus Christ.**

Children of Israel is one of the names of the people God chose to help everyone in the world know God's love. God made a covenant (promise) with the children of Israel, and God is always faithful to his promises.

Fleshpots were sinful or evil places. The Israelites are saying that they would rather return to Egypt with its slavery and sin, because in the desert they are starving while in Egypt they had enough to eat. God comes to their aid and gives them meat (quail) and bread from heaven (manna). God listens to our prayers!

In the Gospel according to Saint John, the miracles that Jesus performs are called signs. When Jesus changes water into wine, or heals someone, or feeds the multitude, he is showing them a sign that he is the Son of God.

To set your seal upon someone is to say that this person is authorized to speak and act on your behalf. It is like a seal of approval or guarantee.

The people in the desert received manna to eat, while Jesus gives us his very self — true bread from heaven. Jesus is the bread of life, and he gives us eternal life.

August 12

19th Sunday in Ordinary Time

A reading from the first book of Kings (19.4-8)

Elijah went a day's journey into the wilderness, and came and sat down under a solitary broom tree. He asked that he might die: "It is enough; now, O Lord, take away my life, for I am no better than my ancestors."

Then Elijah lay down under the broom tree and fell asleep. Suddenly an Angel touched him and said to him, "Get up and eat." He looked, and there at his head was a cake baked on hot stones, and a jar of water. He ate and drank, and lay down again.

The Angel of the Lord came a second time, touched him, and said, "Get up and eat, otherwise the journey will be too much for you." Elijah got up, and ate and drank; then he went in the strength of that food forty days and forty nights to Horeb the mountain of God.

The word of the Lord. **Thanks be to God.**

Psalm 34

R. **Taste and see that the Lord is good.**

I will bless the Lord at all times;
his praise shall continually be in my mouth.
My soul makes its boast in the Lord;
let the humble hear and be glad. R.

O magnify the Lord with me,
and let us exalt his name together.
I sought the Lord, and he answered me,
and delivered me from all my fears. R.

Look to him, and be radiant;
so your faces shall never be ashamed.
The poor one called, and the Lord heard,
and saved that person from every trouble. R.

The Angel of the Lord encamps
around those who fear him, and delivers them.
O taste and see that the Lord is good;
blessed is the one who takes refuge in him. R.

A reading from the Letter of Saint Paul to the Ephesians (4.30 – 5.2)

Brothers and sisters: Do not grieve the Holy Spirit of God, with which you were marked with a seal for the day of redemption. Put away from you all bitterness and wrath and anger and wrangling and slander, together with all malice, and be kind to one another, tender-hearted, forgiving one another, as God in Christ has forgiven you.

Therefore be imitators of God, as beloved children, and live in love, as Christ loved us and gave himself up for us, a fragrant offering and sacrifice to God.

The word of the Lord. **Thanks be to God.**

A reading from the holy Gospel according to John (6.41-51)

The people began to complain about Jesus because he said, "I am the bread that came down from heaven." They were saying, "Is not this Jesus, the son of Joseph, whose father and mother we know? How can he now say, 'I have come down from heaven'?"

Jesus answered them, "Do not complain among yourselves. No one can come to me unless the Father who sent me draw them; and I will raise that person up on the last day. It is written in the Prophets, 'And they shall all be taught by God.' Everyone who has heard and learned from the Father comes to me. Not that anyone has seen the Father except the one who is from God; he has seen the Father. Very truly, I tell you, whoever believes has eternal life.

"I am the bread of life. Your ancestors ate the manna in the wilderness, and they died. This is the bread that comes down from heaven, so that one may eat of it and not die. I am the living bread that came down from heaven. Whoever eats of this bread will live forever; and the bread that I will give for the life of the world is my flesh."

The Gospel of the Lord. **Praise to you, Lord Jesus Christ.**

A broom tree is a kind of tree that grows near the River Jordan and on the Sinai Peninsula. It has a few thin branches and very small leaves, and so gives little shade.

Elijah asks that he might die because he is weary and discouraged, and does not want to continue being a prophet. People were not listening to his message and wanted to kill him. God sent his angel to take care of Elijah by giving him food, drink and, most importantly, hope.

Important events in the history of the people of Israel took place on hilltops or mountains such as Mount Horeb. For example, Moses received the revelation of God's name as well as the Ten Commandments on Mount Sinai; and Jesus was transfigured on a mountain.

We grieve the Holy Spirit of God or make God sad when we do things that set us apart from God and from other people. Although God is much greater than we can ever imagine, Saint Paul tells us to be imitators of God in our daily lives by loving others and walking in God's ways.

We know that Jesus was the son of the Virgin Mary, who became pregnant by the Holy Spirit. People in Jesus' time thought he was the son of Joseph, because Joseph was married to Mary and raised Jesus as his son. Joseph was a descendant of King David, thus fulfilling the prophecy that the Messiah would come from the House of David.

August 19

20th Sunday in Ordinary Time

Wisdom has built her house,
she has hewn her seven pillars.
She has slaughtered her animals,
she has mixed her wine,
she has also set her table.

She has sent out her servant girls,
she calls from the highest places in the town,
"You that are simple, turn in here!"

To those without sense she says,
"Come, eat of my bread
and drink of the wine I have mixed.
Lay aside immaturity, and live,
and walk in the way of insight."

The word of the Lord. **Thanks be to God.**

Psalm 34

R. **Taste and see that the Lord is good.**

I will bless the Lord at all times;
his praise shall continually be in my mouth.
My soul makes its boast in the Lord;
let the humble hear and be glad. R.

O fear the Lord, you his holy ones,
for those who fear him have no want.
The young lions suffer want and hunger,
but those who seek the Lord lack no good thing. R.

Come, O children, listen to me;
I will teach you the fear of the Lord.
Which of you desires life,
and covets many days to enjoy good? R.

Keep your tongue from evil,
and your lips from speaking deceit.
Depart from evil, and do good;
seek peace, and pursue it. R.

Brothers and sisters, be careful how you live, not as unwise people but as wise, making the most of the time, because the days are evil. So do not be foolish, but understand what the will of the Lord is.

Do not get drunk with wine, for that is debauchery; but be filled with the Spirit, as you sing Psalms and hymns and spiritual songs among yourselves, singing and making music to the Lord in your hearts, giving thanks to God the Father at all times and for everything in the name of our Lord Jesus Christ.

The word of the Lord. **Thanks be to God.**

Jesus said to the people: "I am the living bread that came down from heaven. Whoever eats of this bread will live forever; and the bread that I will give for the life of the world is my flesh."

The people then disputed among themselves, saying, "How can this man give us his flesh to eat?"

So Jesus said to them, "Very truly, I tell you, unless you eat the flesh of the Son of Man and drink his blood, you have no life in you. Whoever eats my flesh and drinks my blood has eternal life, and I will raise them up on the last day; for my flesh is true food and my blood is true drink. Whoever eats my flesh and drinks my blood abides in me, and I in them.

"Just as the living Father sent me, and I live because of the Father, so whoever eats me will live because of me. This is the bread that came down from heaven, not like that which your ancestors ate, and they died. But the one who eats this bread will live forever."

The Gospel of the Lord. **Praise to you, Lord Jesus Christ.**

Proverbs is one of the books in the Bible known as wisdom literature. It is a collection of popular sayings and parables filled with everyday advice. Wisdom is characterized as a woman; the Greek word for wisdom is *sophia*.

A Psalm is a prayer that is sung. The book of Psalms in the Bible contains 150 prayers. At every Mass, we recite or sing a Psalm after the first reading. The Liturgy of the Hours (Morning and Evening Prayer) is another beautiful way to learn and sing the Psalms.

Jesus calls himself the living bread because if we accept him and his teachings, we will live with God forever — even after we die. At Mass, we receive his body and blood in the bread and the wine at communion.

When Jesus refers to himself as the Son of Man, he is reminding us of his human nature. The phrase is used in the Hebrew Scriptures or Old Testament to mean a human being. Jesus became a human being so that we might live forever.

The bread that came down from heaven was the manna that God gave the Israelites when they were starving in the desert. The manna helped the people stay alive when food was scarce. Jesus is also bread from heaven, but he is better food than manna because he gives us everlasting life.

21st Sunday in Ordinary Time

Joshua gathered all the tribes of Israel to Shechem, and summoned the elders, the heads, the judges, and the officers of Israel; and they presented themselves before God.

And Joshua said to all the people, "If you are unwilling to serve the Lord, choose this day whom you will serve, whether the gods your ancestors served in the region beyond the River or the gods of the Amorites in whose land you are living. As for me and my household, we will serve the Lord."

Then the people answered, "Far be it from us that we should forsake the Lord to serve other gods; for it is the Lord our God who brought us and our ancestors up from the land of Egypt, out of the house of slavery, and who did those great signs in our sight. He protected us along all the way that we went, and among all the peoples through whom we passed. Therefore we also will serve the Lord, for he is our God."

The word of the Lord. **Thanks be to God.**

Psalm 34

℟ **Taste and see that the Lord is good.**

I will bless the Lord at all times;
his praise shall continually be in my mouth.
My soul makes its boast in the Lord;
let the humble hear and be glad. ℟

The eyes of the Lord are on the righteous,
and his ears are open to their cry.
The face of the Lord is against evildoers,
to cut off the remembrance of them from the earth. ℟

When the righteous cry for help, the Lord hears,
and rescues them from all their troubles.
The Lord is near to the broken-hearted,
and saves the crushed in spirit. ℟

Many are the afflictions of the righteous one,
but the Lord rescues him from them all.
He keeps all his bones;
not one of them will be broken. R.

Evil brings death to the wicked,
and those who hate the righteous will be condemned.
The Lord redeems the life of his servants;
none of those who take refuge in him will be condemned. R.

A reading from the Letter of Saint Paul to the Ephesians (4.32 – 5.1-2, 21-32)

Brothers and sisters: Be kind to one another, tender-hearted, forgiving one another, as God in Christ has forgiven you. Therefore be imitators of God, as beloved children, and live in love, as Christ loved us and gave himself up for us, a fragrant offering and sacrifice to God. Be subject to one another out of reverence for Christ.

Wives, be subject to your husbands as you are to the Lord. For the husband is the head of the wife just as Christ is the head of the Church, the body of which he is the Saviour. Just as the Church is subject to Christ, so also wives ought to be, in everything, to their husbands.

Husbands, love your wives, just as Christ loved the Church and gave himself up for her, in order to make her holy by cleansing her with the washing of water by the word, so as to present the Church to himself in splendour, without a spot or wrinkle or anything of the kind — yes, so that she may be holy and without blemish. In the same way, husbands should love their wives as they do their own bodies. He who loves his wife loves himself. For no one ever hates his own body, but he nourishes and tenderly cares for it, just as Christ does for the Church, because we are members of his body.

For this reason a man will leave his father and mother and be joined to his wife, and the two will become one flesh." This is a great mystery, and I am applying it to Christ and the Church.

The word of the Lord. **Thanks be to God.**

Jesus said to the people: "Very truly, I tell you, unless you eat the flesh of the Son of Man and drink his blood, you have no life in you."

When many of his disciples heard this, they said: "This teaching is difficult; who can accept it?"

But Jesus, being aware that his disciples were complaining about it, said to them, "Does this offend you? Then what if you were to see the Son of Man ascending to where he was before? It is the spirit that gives life; the flesh is useless. The words that I have spoken to you are spirit and life. But among you there are some who do not believe." For Jesus knew from the first who were the ones that did not believe, and who was the one that would betray him.

And he said, "For this reason I have told you that no one can come to me unless it is granted them by my Father."

Because of this many of his disciples turned back, and no longer went about with him. So Jesus asked the twelve, "Do you also wish to go away?"

Simon Peter answered him, "Lord, to whom can we go? You have the words of eternal life. We have come to believe and know that you are the Holy One of God."

The Gospel of the Lord.
**Praise to you,
Lord Jesus Christ.**

After Moses died, God told Joshua to take the people of Israel and conquer the Promised Land. In the Bible, the book of Joshua tells the story of this battle of conquest and describes how the twelve tribes of Israel divided up the land among them.

The Amorites lived in the Promised Land before the Israelites. Many Israelites were attracted by the Amorites' religion and were tempted to leave their own. But Joshua is firm: he and his household will not follow the gods of the Amorites or anyone else, but will worship the one God of Israel.

The Psalms often speak of God as a refuge: a safe place when there is danger. God is always ready to welcome us with open arms, even when we've been less than perfect.

Saint Paul tells the women of his time: be subject to your husbands. He tells the men: love your wives. While we might say it differently, Saint Paul is encouraging husbands and wives to grow in respect and love for each other.

Saint Paul calls marriage a mystery — something wonderful that is hard to understand. Marriage is also a sacrament — an outward sign of God's grace — a vocation to holiness, and a symbol of God's relationship to his people.

The apostles were the twelve close friends who went with Jesus when he was teaching people about God. Jesus later sent them to tell others the good news that God loves us.

22nd Sunday in Ordinary Time

A reading from the book of Deuteronomy (4.1-2, 6-8)

"Now, Israel, give heed to the statutes and ordinances that I am teaching you to observe, so that you may live to enter and occupy the land that the Lord, the God of your fathers, is giving you. You must neither add anything to what I command you nor take away anything from it, but keep the commandments of the Lord your God with which I am charging you.

"You must observe them diligently, for this will show your wisdom and discernment to the peoples, who, when they hear all these statutes, will say, 'Surely this great nation is a wise and discerning people!' For what other great nation has a god so near to it as the Lord our God is whenever we call to him? And what other great nation has statutes and ordinances as just as this entire law that I am setting before you today?"

The word of the Lord. **Thanks be to God.**

Psalm 15

R. **O Lord, who may abide in your tent?**

Whoever walks blamelessly, and does what is right,
and speaks the truth from their heart;
whoever does not slander with their tongue. R.

Whoever does no evil to a friend,
nor takes up a reproach against a neighbour;
in whose eyes the wicked one is despised,
but who honours those who fear the Lord. R.

Whoever stands by their oath even to their hurt;
who does not lend money at interest,
and does not take a bribe against the innocent.
One who does these things shall never be moved. R.

A reading from the Letter of Saint James (1.17-18, 21-22, 27)

Every generous act of giving, with every perfect gift, is from above, coming down from the Father of lights, with whom there is no variation or shadow due to change. In fulfillment of his own purpose he gave us birth by the word of truth, so that we would become a kind of first fruits of his creatures.

Welcome with meekness the implanted word that has the power to save your souls. But be doers of the word, and not merely hearers who deceive themselves.

Religion that is pure and undefiled before God, the Father, is this: to care for orphans and widows in their distress, and to keep oneself unstained by the world.

The word of the Lord. **Thanks be to God.**

A reading from the holy Gospel according to Mark
(7.1-8, 14-15, 21-23)

When the Pharisees and some of the scribes who had come from Jerusalem gathered around Jesus, they noticed that some of his disciples were eating with defiled hands, that is, without washing them. For the Pharisees, and all the Jews, do not eat unless they thoroughly wash their hands, thus observing the tradition of the elders; and they do not eat anything from the market unless they wash it; and there are also many other traditions that they observe, the washing of cups, pots, and bronze kettles. So the Pharisees and the scribes asked him, "Why do your disciples not live according to the tradition of the elders, but eat with defiled hands?"

Jesus said to them, "Isaiah prophesied rightly about you hypocrites, as it is written, 'This people honours me with their lips, but their hearts are far from me; in vain do they worship me, teaching human precepts as doctrines.' You abandon the commandment of God and hold to human tradition."

Then Jesus called the crowd again and said to them, "Listen to me, all of you, and understand: there is nothing outside a person that by going in can defile them, but the things that come out of a person are what defile them.

"For it is from within, from the human heart, that evil intentions come: fornication, theft, murder, adultery, avarice, wickedness, deceit, licentiousness, envy, slander, pride, folly. All these evil things come from within, and they defile a person."

The Gospel of the Lord. **Praise to you, Lord Jesus Christ.**

Deuteronomy is the fifth book in the Hebrew Scriptures or Old Testament. It is a Greek word meaning 'the second law,' or the second time God gave his people his law. It tells us that God is one and so the people of God must be united.

Wisdom is a deep understanding of life. It does not always come with age or from studying many books: it comes from experience and seeing life the way God perceives it.

The Letter of Saint James teaches us that we show our faith both by our words and by our actions, particularly in the way we treat others. We are called as people of faith especially to care for the poor and the oppressed.

When Saint James reminds us to care for orphans and widows, he is speaking about people whom society leaves behind. In the time of Jesus, it was the male head of the household who provided food, security and social standing for the whole family. A widow has no husband, and an orphan no father; neither of them has anyone to protect or provide for them. It is our Christian duty to care for such members of our society.

Hypocrites are people whose actions don't match their words. They may say they love God, but they don't act in a loving way. Such behaviour hurts that person, others around them and God.

September 9

23rd Sunday in Ordinary Time

Say to those who are of a fearful heart,
"Be strong, do not fear!
Here is your God.
He will come with vengeance,
with terrible recompense.
He will come and save you."

Then the eyes of the blind shall be opened,
and the ears of the deaf unstopped;
then the lame shall leap like a deer,
and the tongue of the mute sing for joy.

For waters shall break forth in the wilderness,
and streams in the desert;
the burning sand shall become a pool,
and the thirsty ground springs of water.

The word of the Lord. **Thanks be to God.**

Psalm 146

R. **Praise the Lord, O my soul!**

or **Alleluia!**

It is the Lord who keeps faith forever,
who executes justice for the oppressed;
who gives food to the hungry.
The Lord sets the prisoners free. R.

The Lord opens the eyes of the blind
and lifts up those who are bowed down;
the Lord loves the righteous
and watches over the strangers. R.

The Lord upholds the orphan and the widow,
but the way of the wicked he brings to ruin.
The Lord will reign forever,
your God, O Zion, for all generations. R.

A reading from the Letter of Saint James (2.1-5)

My brothers and sisters, do you with your acts of favouritism really believe in our glorious Lord Jesus Christ? For if a man with gold rings and in fine clothes comes into your assembly, and if a poor person in dirty clothes also comes in, and if you take notice of the one wearing the fine clothes and say, "Have a seat here, please," while to the one who is poor you say, "Stand there," or, "Sit at my feet," have you not made distinctions among yourselves, and become judges with evil thoughts?

Listen, my beloved brothers and sisters. Has not God chosen the poor in the world to be rich in faith and to be heirs of the kingdom that he has promised to those who love him?

The word of the Lord. **Thanks be to God.**

A reading from the holy Gospel according to Mark (7.31-37)

Returning from the region of Tyre, Jesus went by way of Sidon towards the Sea of Galilee, in the region of the Decapolis.

They brought to him a man who was deaf and who had an impediment in his speech; and they begged him to lay his hand on him. Jesus took him aside in private, away from the crowd, and put his fingers into his ears, and he spat and touched his tongue. Then looking up to heaven, he sighed and said to him, "Ephphatha," that is, "Be opened." And immediately the man's ears were opened, his tongue was released, and he spoke plainly.

Then Jesus ordered them to tell no one; but the more he ordered them, the more zealously they proclaimed it. They were astounded beyond measure, saying, "He has done everything well; he even makes the deaf to hear and the mute to speak."

The Gospel of the Lord.
Praise to you, Lord Jesus Christ.

KEY WORDS

People who have a fearful heart feel they are alone and are afraid of everything. Isaiah tells the people not to be afraid, because God is with them. They will find their strength and courage in God.

When Isaiah describes God coming with vengeance (or punishment), he is trying to comfort the people who are afraid. God is on their side; God will bring justice and healing; and God will help set them free.

To keep faith is to honour a promise. God made a promise or covenant with the people of Israel; he also made a New Covenant in Jesus. God always keeps his promises!

Favouritism means treating some people better than others, so that one group gets more than the other. We may find ourselves doing this, but God does not have favourites. God loves all his children equally.

The Bible teaches that every person has dignity, even a poor person. When we ignore the poor and care only for the wealthy, we are turning our back on God. When we treat the poor with kindness and justice, we show our love for Jesus.

Decapolis is a Greek word meaning 'ten cities.' This group of cities was near where Jesus lived. See the map on page 320.

Often when Jesus healed people, he would lay his hand on their heads. This gesture is now part of certain sacraments, such as confirmation and holy orders (priesthood). It is a sign that the power of God, the Holy Spirit, is being given to the person.

24th Sunday in Ordinary Time

A reading from the book of the Prophet Isaiah (50.5-9)

The Lord God has opened my ear,
and I was not rebellious,
I did not turn backward.
I gave my back to those who struck me,
and my cheeks to those who pulled out the beard;
I did not hide my face from insult and spitting.
The Lord God helps me; therefore I have not been disgraced;
therefore I have set my face like flint,
and I know that I shall not be put to shame;
he who vindicates me is near.
Who will contend with me? Let us stand up together.
Who are my adversaries? Let them confront me.

It is the Lord God who helps me; who will declare me guilty?

The word of the Lord. **Thanks be to God.**

Psalm 116

R. **I will walk before the Lord, in the land of the living.**
or **Alleluia!**

I love the Lord, because he has heard
my voice and my supplications.
Because he inclined his ear to me,
therefore I will call on him as long as I live. R.

The snares of death encompassed me;
the pangs of Sheol laid hold on me;
I suffered distress and anguish.
Then I called on the name of the Lord:
"O Lord, I pray, save my life!" R.

Gracious is the Lord, and righteous;
our God is merciful.
The Lord protects the simple;
when I was brought low, he saved me. R.

For you have delivered my soul from death,
my eyes from tears, my feet from stumbling.
I will walk before the Lord
in the land of the living. R.

A reading from the Letter of Saint James (2.14-18)

What good is it, my brothers and sisters, if you say you have faith but do not have works? Can faith save you?

If a brother or a sister is without clothing and lacks daily food, and one of you says to them, "Go in peace; keep warm and eat your fill," and yet you do not supply their bodily needs, what is the good of that? So faith by itself, if it has no works, is dead.

But someone will say, "You have faith and I have works." Show me your faith apart from your works, and I by my works will show you my faith.

The word of the Lord. **Thanks be to God.**

A reading from the holy Gospel according to Mark (8.27-35)

Jesus went on with his disciples to the villages of Caesarea Philippi; and on the way he asked his disciples, "Who do people say that I am?" And they answered him, "John the Baptist; and others, Elijah; and still others, one of the Prophets."

Jesus asked them, "But who do you say that I am?" Peter answered him, "You are the Christ." And he sternly ordered them not to tell anyone about him.

Then he began to teach them that the Son of Man must undergo great suffering, and be rejected by the elders, the chief priests, and the scribes, and be killed, and after three days rise again. He said all this quite openly.

And Peter took Jesus aside and began to rebuke him. But turning and looking at his disciples, he rebuked Peter and said, "Get behind me, Satan! For you are thinking not as God does, but as humans do."

Jesus called the crowd with his disciples, and said to them, "Whoever wants to become my follower, let him deny himself and take up his cross and follow me. For whoever wants to save their life will lose it, and whoever loses their life for my sake, and for the sake of the Gospel, will save it."

The Gospel of the Lord. **Praise to you, Lord Jesus Christ.**

To vindicate someone means to defend them when they are being treated unfairly. Isaiah knows he can stand with courage and hope because God is at his side.

Saint James' teaching in his letter is important for everyone. He shows us that it is not what we say that proves our belief; faith shows itself in works or deeds that prove we are living the way Jesus taught us to live.

John the Baptist was the son of Zechariah and Elizabeth, and the cousin of Jesus. He prepared the way for Jesus, telling the people that the Messiah, Jesus, was coming. He is called the Baptist because he baptized people as a sign of their willingness to change their lives. He was a great prophet.

Satan is one of the names given to the enemy of God and our strongest enemy. Satan works against God and tries to lead people away from God's love. In today's Gospel, when Peter argues with Jesus over whether it is necessary for Jesus to die, Jesus calls Peter "Satan" because Peter wants to reject God's will that Jesus should suffer, die and be raised from the dead.

When Jesus says whoever wants to be his follower must take up his cross, he is challenging us to accept everything that comes with being Christian. We proudly mark ourselves with the sign of the cross, and we accept whatever comes our way as a result. We must be prepared to let go of our life if we want to save our life.

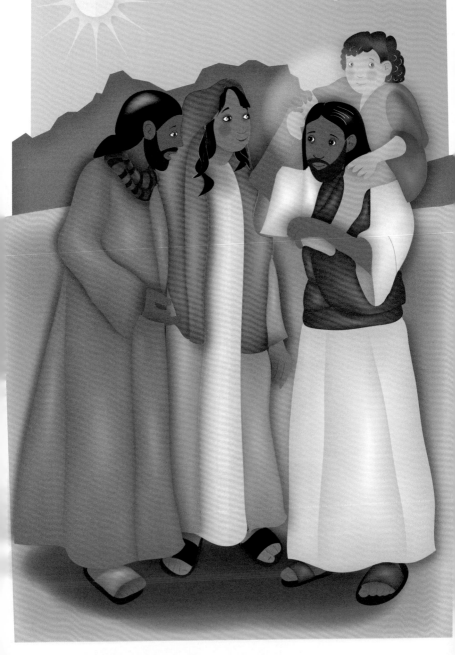

September 23

25th Sunday in Ordinary Time

The godless say, "Let us lie in wait for the righteous one, who makes life inconvenient to us and opposes our actions; who reproaches us for sins against the law, and accuses us of sins against our training.

"Let us see if his words are true, and let us test what will happen at the end of his life; for if the righteous one is God's son, God will help him, and will deliver him from the hand of his adversaries.

"Let us test him with insult and torture, so that we may find out how gentle he is, and make trial of his forbearance. Let us condemn him to a shameful death, for, according to what he says, he will be protected."

The word of the Lord. **Thanks be to God.**

Psalm 54

R. **The Lord upholds my life.**

Save me, O God, by your name,
and vindicate me by your might.
Hear my prayer, O God;
give ear to the words of my mouth. R.

For the insolent have risen against me,
the ruthless seek my life;
they do not set God before them. R.

But surely, God is my helper;
the Lord is the upholder of my life.
With a freewill offering I will sacrifice to you;
I will give thanks to your name, for it is good. R.

A reading from the Letter of Saint James (3.16 – 4.3)

Beloved: Where there is envy and selfish ambition, there will also be disorder and wickedness of every kind. But the wisdom from above is first pure, then peaceable, gentle, willing to yield, full of mercy and good fruits, without a trace of partiality or hypocrisy. And a harvest of righteousness is sown in peace for those who make peace.

Those conflicts and disputes among you, where do they come from? Do they not come from your cravings that are at war within you? You want something and do not have it; so you commit murder. And you covet something and cannot obtain it; so you engage in disputes and conflicts.

You do not have, because you do not ask. You ask and do not receive, because you ask wrongly, in order to spend what you get on your pleasures.

The word of the Lord. **Thanks be to God.**

A reading from the holy Gospel according to Mark (9.30-37)

After leaving the mountain Jesus and his disciples went on from there and passed through Galilee. He did not want anyone to know it; for he was teaching his disciples, saying to them, "The Son of Man is to be betrayed into the hands of men, and they will kill him, and three days after being killed, he will rise again." But they did not understand what he was saying and were afraid to ask him.

Then they came to Capernaum; and when he was in the house Jesus asked them, "What were you arguing about on the way?" But they were silent, for on the way they had argued with one another who was the greatest.

Jesus sat down, called the twelve, and said to them, "Whoever wants to be first must be last of all and servant of all."

Then he took a little child and put it among them; and taking it in his arms, he said to them, "Whoever welcomes one such child in my name welcomes me, and whoever welcomes me welcomes not me but the one who sent me."

The Gospel of the Lord. **Praise to you, Lord Jesus Christ.**

The book of Wisdom was written not long before Jesus was born. It is one of seven biblical books called wisdom literature (the others are Job, Psalms, Proverbs, Ecclesiastes, Song of Solomon, and Sirach). It urges God's people to stand firm in faith, even when life is difficult or hostile.

Mercy is God's loving concern for everyone, but most especially for the poor and the weak. Saint James lists mercy as one of the characteristics of heavenly wisdom: if we truly are God's children, then we will be merciful as God is merciful.

Disputes and conflicts happen when people think only of themselves and not of the needs of others. These arguments prevent the community from growing together in love. If we are to make peace, as Saint James says, we must first live in a peaceable manner.

Capernaum was a fishing village on the north shore of the Sea of Galilee (see the map, page 320). Jesus frequently taught in Capernaum and performed miracles there.

Young children are defenceless and depend on adults to care for them. This Gospel shows how important each child is to God. Jesus says that when we welcome children, we welcome Jesus and God his Father.

September 30

26th Sunday in Ordinary Time

The Lord came down in the cloud, took some of the spirit that was on Moses and put it on the seventy elders. When the spirit rested upon them, they prophesied. But they did not do so again.

Two men remained in the camp, one named Eldad, and the other named Medad, and the spirit rested on them; they were among those registered, but they had not gone out to the tent, and so they prophesied in the camp. A young man ran and told Moses, "Eldad and Medad are prophesying in the camp."

Joshua son of Nun, the assistant of Moses, one of his chosen men, said, "My lord Moses, stop them!" But Moses said to him, "Are you jealous for my sake? Would that all the Lord's people were Prophets, and that the Lord would put his spirit on them!"

The word of the Lord. **Thanks be to God.**

Psalm 19

R̰ **The precepts of the Lord are right,**
and give joy to the heart.

The law of the Lord is perfect,
reviving the soul;
the decrees of the Lord are sure,
making wise the simple. R̰

The fear of the Lord is pure,
enduring forever;
the ordinances of the Lord are true
and righteous altogether. R̰

By them is your servant warned;
in keeping them there is great reward.
But who can detect unmindful errors?
Clear me from hidden faults. R̰

Keep back your servant also from the insolent;
do not let them have dominion over me.
Then I shall be blameless,
and innocent of great transgression. R̰

A reading from the Letter of Saint James (5.1-6)

Come now, you rich people, weep and wail for the miseries that are coming to you. Your riches have rotted, and your clothes are moth-eaten. Your gold and silver have rusted, and their rust will be evidence against you, and it will eat your flesh like fire.

You have laid up treasure for the last days. Listen! The wages of the labourers who mowed your fields, which you kept back by fraud, cry out, and the cries of the harvesters have reached the ears of the Lord of hosts.

You have lived on the earth in luxury and in pleasure; you have fattened your hearts in a day of slaughter. You have condemned and murdered the righteous one, who does not resist you.

The word of the Lord. **Thanks be to God.**

A reading from the holy Gospel according to Mark (9.38-43, 45, 47-48)

After Jesus had finished teaching the disciples, John said to him, "Teacher, we saw someone casting out demons in your name, and we tried to stop him, because he was not following us." But Jesus said, "Do not stop him; for no one who does a deed of power in my name will be able soon afterward to speak evil of me. Whoever is not against us is for us.

"For truly I tell you, whoever gives you a cup of water to drink because you bear the name of Christ will by no means lose the reward.

"If any of you put a stumbling block before one of these little ones who believe in me, it would be better for you if a great millstone were hung around your neck and you were thrown into the sea.

"If your hand causes you to stumble, cut it off; it is better for you to enter life maimed than to have two hands and to go to hell, to the unquenchable fire. And if your foot causes you to stumble, cut it off; it is better for you to enter life lame than to have two feet and to be thrown into hell. And if your eye causes you to stumble, tear it out; it is better for you to enter the kingdom of God with one eye than to have two eyes and to be thrown into hell, where their worm never dies, and the fire is never quenched."

The Gospel of the Lord. **Praise to you, Lord Jesus Christ.**

248

The book of Numbers is found in the Hebrew Scriptures or Old Testament. It is called "Numbers" because it talks about many numbers and times when the people of Israel were counted. In Hebrew, it is called "In the Desert," because it tells of the travels of the Israelites, after they left slavery in Egypt.

To prophesy can sometimes mean to announce what is going to happen in the future. In the Bible, however, prophets speak for God, reminding the people of God's promises and their own need to remain faithful to the covenant.

Joshua helped Moses lead the people of Israel to the Promised Land. Moses died before they got there, and so Joshua became the leader of the Israelites as they conquered the land. He is the central person in the book of Joshua.

Fraud is stealing or lying so that you can gain at another person's expense. A just and fair employer does not defraud employees, but rather pays them all that is owed to them.

When Jesus tells people to cut off their hand or their foot if it is causing them to sin, he means we must sometimes let go of valuable things in order to obey God. No one should cut off a part of their body, unless it is to save their lives.

October 7

27th Sunday in Ordinary Time

The Lord God formed man from the dust of the ground, and breathed into his nostrils the breath of life, and put him in the garden of Eden to till it and keep it.

Then the Lord God said, "It is not good that the man should be alone; I will make him a helper as his partner." So out of the ground the Lord God formed every animal of the field and every bird of the air, and brought them to the man to see what he would call them; and whatever the man called every living creature, that was its name. The man gave names to all cattle, and to the birds of the air, and to every animal of the field; but for the man there was not found a helper as his partner.

So the Lord God caused a deep sleep to fall upon the man, and he slept; then he took one of his ribs and closed up its place with flesh. And the rib that the Lord God had taken from the man he made into a woman and brought her to the man.

Then the man said, "This at last is bone of my bones and flesh of my flesh; this one shall be called Woman, for out of Man this one was taken."

Therefore a man leaves his father and his mother and clings to his wife, and they become one flesh.

The word of the Lord. **Thanks be to God.**

Psalm 128

R. **May the Lord bless us all the days of our lives.**

Blessed is everyone who fears the Lord,
who walks in his ways.
You shall eat the fruit of the labour of your hands;
you shall be happy, and it shall go well with you. R.

Your wife will be like a fruitful vine
within your house;
your children will be like olive shoots
around your table. R.

Thus shall the man be blessed who fears the Lord.
The Lord bless you from Zion.
May you see the prosperity of Jerusalem
all the days of your life. R.

A reading from the Letter to the Hebrews (2.9-11)

We do indeed see Jesus, who for a little while was made lower than the Angels, now crowned with glory and honour because of the suffering of death, so that by the grace of God he might taste death for everyone.

It was fitting that God, for whom and through whom all things exist, in bringing many sons and daughters to glory should make the pioneer of their salvation perfect through sufferings. For the one who sanctifies and those who are sanctified are all from one. For this reason he is not ashamed to call them brothers and sisters.

The word of the Lord. **Thanks be to God.**

A reading from the holy Gospel according to Mark (10.2-16)

The shorter version ends at the asterisks.

Some Pharisees came, and to test Jesus they asked, "Is it lawful for a man to divorce his wife?" Jesus answered them, "What did Moses command you?" They said, "Moses allowed a man to write a certificate of dismissal and to divorce her."

But Jesus said to them, "Because of your hardness of heart he wrote this commandment for you. But from the beginning of creation, 'God made them male and female.' 'For this reason a man shall leave his father and mother and be joined to his wife, and the two shall become one flesh.' So they are no longer two, but one flesh. Therefore what God has joined together, let no one separate."

Then in the house the disciples asked him again about this matter. Jesus said to them, "Whoever divorces his wife and marries another commits adultery against her; and if she divorces her husband and marries another, she commits adultery."

* * *

People were bringing little children to him in order that Jesus might touch them; and the disciples spoke sternly to them. But when Jesus saw this, he was indignant and said to them, "Let the little children come to me; do not stop them: for it is to such as these that the kingdom of God belongs. Truly I tell you, whoever does not receive the kingdom of God as a little child will never enter it."

And Jesus took them up in his arms, laid his hands on them, and blessed them.

The Gospel of the Lord. **Praise to you, Lord Jesus Christ.**

The man (in Hebrew, *adam*) is the name that the book of Genesis gives to the first human being God created from the earth (in Hebrew, *adama*). We call him Adam. The first woman was called Eve ('living one').

In the Bible, to name something is to be responsible for it. God let Adam name the animals he created. It was then Adam's job to take care of them. We are all asked to care for God's creation.

When God takes one of the man's ribs to form a woman, God shows that women and men share the same human nature. God wants us to work side by side to care for the world and each other.

The writer of the Letter to the Hebrews, in today's reading, is speaking about the order of beings in heaven. The angels are close to God, but Jesus is the closest. In becoming human, Jesus lowered himself below the angels; but after his resurrection, he was crowned with glory and honour and returned to his rightful place with God.

The law that was given to Moses allowed divorce, but Jesus teaches that when a man and a woman are joined in God's eyes in marriage, their love never ends and they cannot be separated until death. In the Catholic Church, marriage is a sacrament — an outward sign of God's grace and a vocation to holiness.

28th Sunday in Ordinary Time

I prayed, and understanding was given me;
I called on God, and the spirit of wisdom came to me.

I preferred her to sceptres and thrones,
and I accounted wealth as nothing in comparison with her.
Neither did I liken to her any priceless gem,
because all gold is but a little sand in her sight,
and silver will be accounted as clay before her.

I loved her more than health and beauty,
and I chose to have her rather than light,
because her radiance never ceases.
All good things came to me along with her,
and in her hands uncounted wealth.

The word of the Lord. **Thanks be to God.**

Psalm 90

R. **Fill us with your love, O Lord,
that we may rejoice and be glad.**

Teach us to count our days
that we may gain a wise heart.
Turn, O Lord! How long?
Have compassion on your servants! R.

Satisfy us in the morning with your steadfast love,
so that we may rejoice and be glad all our days.
Make us glad as many days as you have afflicted us,
and as many years as we have seen evil. R.

Let your work be manifest to your servants,
and your glorious power to their children.
Let the favour of the Lord our God be upon us,
and prosper for us the work of our hands. R.

A reading from the Letter to the Hebrews (4.12-13)

The word of God is living and active, sharper than any two-edged sword, piercing until it divides soul from spirit, joints from marrow; it is able to judge the thoughts and intentions of the heart.

And before God no creature is hidden, but all are naked and laid bare to the eyes of the one to whom we must render an account.

The word of the Lord. **Thanks be to God.**

A reading from the holy Gospel according to Mark (10.17-30)

The shorter version ends at the asterisks.

As Jesus was setting out on a journey, a man ran up and knelt before him, and asked him, "Good Teacher, what must I do to inherit eternal life?"

Jesus said to him, "Why do you call me good? No one is good but God alone. You know the commandments: 'You shall not murder; You shall not commit adultery; You shall not steal; You shall not bear false witness; You shall not defraud; Honour your father and mother.'"

He said to Jesus, "Teacher, I have kept all these since my youth." Jesus, looking at him, loved him and said, "You lack one thing; go, sell what you own, and give the money to the poor, and you will have treasure in heaven; then come, follow me."

When the man heard this, he was shocked and went away grieving, for he had many possessions.

Then Jesus looked around and said to his disciples, "How hard it will be for those who have wealth to enter the kingdom of God!" And the disciples were perplexed at these words. But Jesus said to them again, "Children, how hard it is to enter the kingdom of God! It is easier for a camel to go through the eye of a needle than for someone who is rich to enter the kingdom of God."

They were greatly astounded and said to one another, "Then who can be saved?" Jesus looked at them and said, "For humans it is impossible, but not for God; for God all things are possible."

* * *

Peter began to say to him, "Look, we have left everything and followed you." Jesus said, "Truly I tell you, there is no one who has left house or brothers or sisters or mother or father or children or fields, for my sake and for the sake of the good news, who will not receive a hundredfold now in this age — houses, brothers and sisters, mothers and children, and fields — but with persecutions — and in the age to come, eternal life."

The Gospel of the Lord.
**Praise to you,
Lord Jesus Christ.**

Wisdom is a deep understanding of life. It does not always come with age or from studying many books: it comes from experience. Wisdom is one of the seven gifts of the Holy Spirit — it allows us to see God in everyone and everything around us.

Sceptres and thrones are two signs of a king or queen's power. A sceptre is a fancy wand they hold in their hand. It represents authority. The Bible says it is better to have wisdom than to have worldly power.

When we kneel before someone, we are showing reverence and obedience to that person. In today's Gospel, the man knelt before Jesus because he believed Jesus to be a great teacher deserving of his respect.

When Jesus says to the rich man, "Come, follow me," he is also inviting us to follow him: sharing the good news of God's love with everyone, and sharing our wealth with the poor.

When we are grieving, we are sad because we have lost someone or something important to us. The young man was saddened by the thought of giving up his belongings — but he might also have been sad because he wasn't strong enough to leave his possessions and follow Jesus.

The eye of a needle is the opening at the top of a needle through which thread is looped. Surely it is impossible for a camel to pass through the eye! By using this saying, Jesus is showing us that we have no other option: we must not merely think about giving to the poor, we must actually do it, if we are to have eternal life.

October 21

29th Sunday in Ordinary Time

It was the will of the Lord to crush him with pain. When you make his life an offering for sin, he shall see his offspring, and shall prolong his days; through him the will of the Lord shall prosper. Out of his anguish he shall see light; he shall find satisfaction through his knowledge. The righteous one, my servant, shall make many righteous, and he shall bear their iniquities.

The word of the Lord. **Thanks be to God.**

Psalm 33

R. Let your love be upon on us, Lord, even as we hope in you.

The word of the Lord is upright,
and all his work is done in faithfulness.
He loves righteousness and justice;
the earth is full of the steadfast love of the Lord. R.

Truly the eye of the Lord is on those who fear him,
on those who hope in his steadfast love,
to deliver their soul from death,
and to keep them alive in famine. R.

Our soul waits for the Lord;
he is our help and shield.
Let your steadfast love, O Lord, be upon us,
even as we hope in you. R.

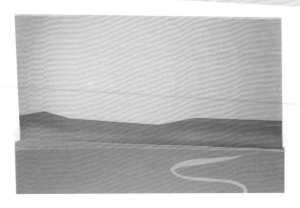

A reading from the Letter to the Hebrews (4.14-16)

Brothers and sisters: Since we have a great high priest who has passed through the heavens, Jesus, the Son of God, let us hold fast to our confession. For we do not have a high priest who is unable to sympathize with our weaknesses, but we have one who in every respect has been tested as we are, yet without sin.

Let us therefore approach the throne of grace with boldness, so that we may receive mercy and find grace to help in time of need.

The word of the Lord. **Thanks be to God.**

A reading from the holy Gospel according to Mark (10.35-45)

The shorter version begins at the asterisks.

James and John, the sons of Zebedee, came forward to Jesus and said to him, "Teacher, we want you to do for us whatever we ask of you." And Jesus said to them, "What is it you want me to do for you?" And they said to him, "Grant us to sit, one at your right hand and one at your left, in your glory."

But Jesus said to them, "You do not know what you are asking. Are you able to drink the cup that I drink, or be baptized with the baptism that I am baptized with?" They replied, "We are able."

Then Jesus said to them, "The cup that I drink you will drink; and with the baptism with which I am baptized, you will be baptized; but to sit at my right hand or at my left is not mine to grant, but it is for those for whom it has been prepared."

When the ten heard this, they began to be angry with James and John.

* * *

So Jesus called them and said to them, "You know that among the Gentiles those whom they recognize as their rulers lord it over them, and their great ones are tyrants over them. But it is not so among you; whoever wishes to become great among you must be your servant, and whoever wishes to be first among you must be slave of all. For the Son of Man came not to be served but to serve, and to give his life as a ransom for many."

The Gospel of the Lord. **Praise to you, Lord Jesus Christ.**

Offspring are children and grandchildren. They were very important to the Jewish people, because they carried the faith of the people into the future. To have many children was a sign of God's blessing. In the book of Isaiah, the person who is suffering will be blessed by God: he will live to see his children for many days.

Anguish is great mental or physical pain. Isaiah tells us that people who suffer will gain wisdom from their experience and will one day find peace. We can trust in God to help us endure our pain.

In the Hebrew Scriptures or Old Testament, righteousness means following the laws Moses gave to the people of Israel. Righteousness is a gift God gives all of his people through Christ.

Famine is a period of time when there is not enough food in a country. The people go hungry day after day. Floods, drought, insects or war are some reasons crops cannot grow. The Psalmist trusts that God will keep his people alive in time of famine.

Mercy is God's loving forgiveness of our sins. God is always merciful. At the beginning of Mass we say, "Lord, have mercy; Christ, have mercy; Lord, have mercy," both to ask for God's mercy and to remind us of how merciful God is.

The Gentiles were non-Jewish people. Their faith, government and customs were different from those of the Jewish people. Jesus tells his disciples not to act like the leaders of the Gentiles, who do not always treat their people fairly.

Ransom is a sum of money or other valuable thing that is paid to save someone's life or to free a prisoner. Jesus gave the most valuable thing he had — his life — in order to ransom or save everyone from sin and death. He chose to do this because he loves us.

October 28

30th Sunday in Ordinary Time

Thus says the Lord:
"Sing aloud with gladness for Jacob,
and raise shouts for the chief of the nations;
proclaim, give praise, and say,
'Save, O Lord, your people,
the remnant of Israel.'
"See, I am going to bring them from the land of the north,
and gather them from the farthest parts of the earth,
among them those who are blind and those who are lame,
those with child and those in labour, together;
a great company, they shall return here.
"With weeping they shall come,
and with consolations I will lead them back,
I will let them walk by brooks of water,
in a straight path in which they shall not stumble;
for I have become a father to Israel,
and Ephraim is my firstborn."
The word of the Lord. **Thanks be to God.**

Psalm 126

R. **The Lord has done great things for us;
we are filled with joy.**

When the Lord restored the fortunes of Zion,
we were like those who dream.
Then our mouth was filled with laughter,
and our tongue with shouts of joy. R.

Then it was said among the nations,
"The Lord has done great things for them."
The Lord has done great things for us,
and we rejoiced. R.

Restore our fortunes, O Lord,
like the watercourses in the desert of the Negev.
May those who sow in tears
reap with shouts of joy. R.

Those who go out weeping,
bearing the seed for sowing,
shall come home with shouts of joy,
carrying their sheaves. R.

A reading from the Letter to the Hebrews (5.1-6)

Every high priest chosen from among men is put in charge of things pertaining to God on their behalf, to offer gifts and sacrifices for sins. He is able to deal gently with the ignorant and wayward, since he himself is subject to weakness; and because of this he must offer sacrifice for his own sins as well as for those of the people. And one does not presume to take this honour, but takes it only when called by God, just as Aaron was.

So also Christ did not glorify himself in becoming a high priest, but was appointed by the one who said to him, "You are my Son, today I have begotten you"; as he says also in another place, "You are a priest forever, according to the order of Melchizedek."

The word of the Lord. **Thanks be to God.**

A reading from the holy Gospel according to Mark (10.46-52)

As Jesus and his disciples and a large crowd were leaving Jericho, Bartimaeus son of Timaeus, a blind beggar, was sitting by the roadside. When he heard that it was Jesus of Nazareth, he began to shout out and say, "Jesus, Son of David, have mercy on me!" Many sternly ordered him to be quiet, but he cried out even more loudly, "Son of David, have mercy on me!"

Jesus stood still and said, "Call him here." And they called the blind man, saying to him, "Take heart; get up, he is calling you." So throwing off his cloak, he sprang up and came to Jesus.

Then Jesus said to him, "What do you want me to do for you?" The blind man said to him, "My teacher, let me see again." Jesus said to him, "Go; your faith has made you well."

Immediately the man regained his sight and followed Jesus on the way.

The Gospel of the Lord. **Praise to you, Lord Jesus Christ.**

Jacob was the grandson of Abraham and the father of many children. His twelve sons were the first leaders of the twelve tribes of the Jewish people. In this reading, Jacob represents all of the people of Israel.

Ephraim was a son of Joseph (one of Jacob's sons) who was later adopted by Jacob and became the head of one of the twelve tribes of Israel. The Bible sometimes uses the name Ephraim to mean the whole people of Israel.

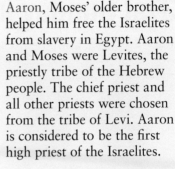

Aaron, Moses' older brother, helped him free the Israelites from slavery in Egypt. Aaron and Moses were Levites, the priestly tribe of the Hebrew people. The chief priest and all other priests were chosen from the tribe of Levi. Aaron is considered to be the first high priest of the Israelites.

Son of David (or descendant of King David) is a name the Hebrew people used to describe the Messiah. They were expecting the Messiah to be born of the House of David. In today's Gospel, Bartimaeus knows in his heart that the person who is passing by is the Messiah, so he calls Jesus "Son of David."

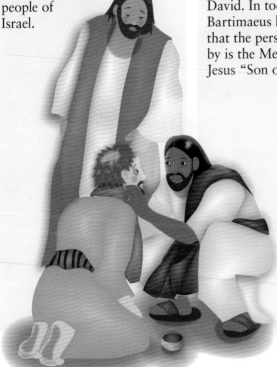

31st Sunday in Ordinary Time

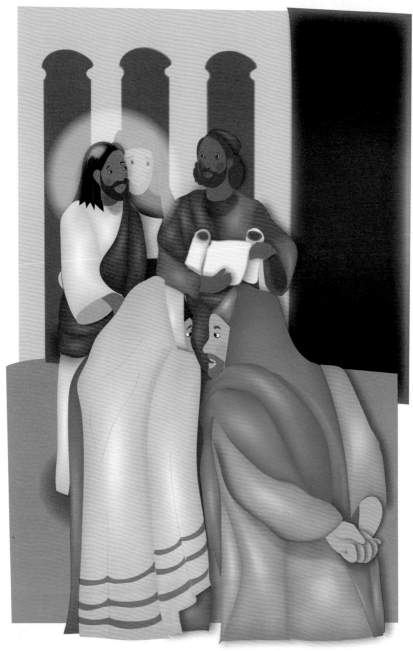

Moses spoke to the people: "May you and your children and your children's children fear the Lord your God all the days of your life, and keep all his decrees and his commandments that I am commanding you, so that your days may be long.

"Hear therefore, O Israel, and observe them diligently, so that it may go well with you, and so that you may multiply greatly in a land flowing with milk and honey, as the Lord, the God of your Fathers, has promised you.

"Hear, O Israel: The Lord is our God, the Lord alone. You shall love the Lord your God with all your heart, and with all your soul, and with all your might. Keep these words that I am commanding you today in your heart."

The word of the Lord. **Thanks be to God.**

Psalm 18

R. **I love you, O Lord, my strength.**

I love you, O Lord, my strength.
The Lord is my rock, my fortress, and my deliverer.
My God, my rock in whom I take refuge,
my shield, and the source of my salvation, my stronghold. R.

I call upon the Lord, who is worthy to be praised,
so I shall be saved from my enemies.
From his temple he heard my voice,
and my cry to him reached his ears. R.

The Lord lives! Blessed be my rock,
and exalted be the God of my salvation.
Great triumphs he gives to his king,
and shows steadfast love to his anointed. R.

A reading from the Letter to the Hebrews (7.23-28)

The priests of the first covenant were many in number, because they were prevented by death from continuing in office; but Jesus holds his priesthood permanently, because he continues forever. Consequently he is able for all time to save those who approach God through him, since he always lives to make intercession for them.

For it was fitting that we should have such a high priest, holy, blameless, undefiled, separated from sinners, and exalted above the heavens. Unlike the other high priests, he has no need to offer sacrifices day after day, first for his own sins, and then for those of the people; this he did once for all when he offered himself.

For the law appoints as high priests those who are subject to weakness, but the word of the oath, which came later than the law, appoints a Son who has been made perfect forever.

The word of the Lord. **Thanks be to God.**

A reading from the holy Gospel according to Mark (12.28-34)

One of the scribes came near and heard the religious authorities disputing with one another, and seeing that Jesus answered them well, he asked him, "Which commandment is the first of all?"

Jesus answered, "The first is, 'Hear, O Israel: the Lord our God, the Lord is one; you shall love the Lord your God with all your heart, and with all your soul, and with all your mind, and with all your strength.' The second is this, 'You shall love your neighbour as yourself.' There is no other commandment greater than these."

Then the scribe said to him, "You are right, Teacher; you have truly said that 'he is one, and besides him there is no other'; and 'to love him with all the heart, and with all the understanding, and with all the strength,' and 'to love one's neighbour as oneself,' — this is much more important than all whole burnt offerings and sacrifices."

When Jesus saw that the scribe answered wisely, he said to him, "You are not far from the kingdom of God."

After that no one dared to ask Jesus any question.

The Gospel of the Lord. **Praise to you, Lord Jesus Christ.**

A land flowing with milk and honey is rich and fertile. There is abundant water and plant life for grazing sheep and goats, as well as fruits and vegetables. The animals provide milk, and the plants and trees are key for the production of honey and syrups. For a people without a fixed home, this is indeed paradise!

The high priest was the chief of all the priests, who were the mediators between God and his people. When the high priest died, his son became high priest after him. In the Letter to the Hebrews, the writer shows us how Jesus, as both God and a human being, is the perfect high priest, interceding for us with God. There is no need for another, for Jesus is our high priest forever.

In Jesus' time, scribes wrote letters and kept records for the community. The word 'scribe' comes from the Latin *scribere*, 'to write'. They also studied the Law of Moses. In the gospels, scribes often asked Jesus hard questions. This was how they learned and tested their knowledge of the Law.

A burnt offering is a sacrifice to God made in the temple, where a whole animal was offered on the fire. It was the highest form of sacrifice, since the animal was wholly consumed by fire and nothing was left over. The scribe in today's Gospel acknowledges that Jesus has indeed spoken the greatest commandment — it is more important to love God and our neighbour than it is to give the highest sacrifice.

32nd Sunday in Ordinary Time

Elijah, the Prophet, set out and went to Zarephath. When he came to the gate of the town, a widow was there gathering sticks; he called to her and said, "Bring me a little water in a vessel, so that I may drink." As she was going to bring it, he called to her and said, "Bring me a morsel of bread in your hand."

But she said, "As the Lord your God lives, I have nothing baked, only a handful of meal in a jar, and a little oil in a jug; I am now gathering a couple of sticks, so that I may go home and prepare it for myself and my son, that we may eat it, and die."

Elijah said to her, "Do not be afraid; go and do as you have said; but first make me a little cake of it and bring it to me, and afterwards make something for yourself and your son. For thus says the Lord the God of Israel: 'The jar of meal will not be emptied and the jug of oil will not fail until the day that the Lord sends rain on the earth.'"

She went and did as Elijah said, so that she as well as he and her household ate for many days. The jar of meal was not emptied, neither did the jug of oil fail, according to the word of the Lord that he spoke by Elijah.

The word of the Lord. **Thanks be to God.**

Psalm 146

R. **Praise the Lord, O my soul!**

or **Alleluia!**

It is the Lord who keeps faith forever,
who executes justice for the oppressed;
who gives food to the hungry.
The Lord sets the prisoners free. R.

The Lord opens the eyes of the blind
and lifts up those who are bowed down;
the Lord loves the righteous
and watches over the strangers. R.

The Lord upholds the orphan and the widow,
but the way of the wicked he brings to ruin.
The Lord will reign forever,
your God, O Zion, for all generations. R.

Christ did not enter a sanctuary made by human hands, a mere copy of the true one, but he entered into heaven itself, now to appear in the presence of God on our behalf.

Nor was it to offer himself again and again, as the high priest enters the Holy Place year after year with blood that is not his own; for then he would have had to suffer again and again since the foundation of the world.

But as it is, he has appeared once for all at the end of the age to remove sin by the sacrifice of himself. And just as it is appointed for human beings to die once, and after that comes the judgment, so Christ, having been offered once to bear the sins of many, will appear a second time, not to deal with sin, but to save those who are eagerly waiting for him.

The word of the Lord. **Thanks be to God.**

The shorter version begins at the asterisks.

Jesus was teaching in the temple, and a large crowd was listening to him. He said, "Beware of the scribes, who like to walk around in long robes, and to be greeted with respect in the marketplaces, and to have the best seats in the synagogues and places of honour at banquets! They devour widows' houses and for the sake of appearance say long prayers. They will receive the greater condemnation."

* * *

Jesus sat down opposite the treasury, and watched the crowd putting money into the treasury. Many rich people put in large sums. A poor widow came and put in two small copper coins, which are worth a penny. Then he called his disciples and said to them, "Truly I tell you, this poor widow has put in more than all those who are contributing to the treasury. For all of them have contributed out of their abundance; but she out of her poverty has put in everything she had, all she had to live on."

The Gospel of the Lord. **Praise to you, Lord Jesus Christ.**

Meal is a word for grain that is ground up into flour for making bread. The widow in Zarephath uses the last bit of meal in her jar to feed Elijah, God's prophet. God rewards her selflessness by making a miracle happen — her jar of meal never runs out!

The oppressed are people who are treated unfairly by others. God never forgets the oppressed and desires their freedom from oppression. There are many oppressed people in our world today. When we work to help the oppressed, we are working with God to set them free.

Zion was the name of a hill in Jerusalem, where the temple was built. Sometimes the entire city was called Zion. The name Zion can also mean the whole people of Israel.

A sanctuary is a holy place in a temple or church. In a temple, it is where the Ark of the Covenant is kept. In Catholic churches, it is where the altar and tabernacle are found. In heaven, Jesus appears before God in the heavenly sanctuary to intercede for us as our high priest.

The treasury was the place where people gave money for the upkeep of the temple. It is similar to the collection that is taken up at each Mass in our day.

A widow is a woman whose husband has died. A widow in Israel had no one to care for her. God made a law saying that the people of Israel had to care for widows and orphans (children whose parents have died). In today's Gospel, a widow gives as much as she can to the temple in Jerusalem. Even though she is poor, she is generous towards God because she loves God and recognizes how good God is to her.

To have in abundance means to have more than enough. Jesus noticed that many people gave to the temple treasury from their extra money, not from the money they used for their basic needs. To be generous means to give from our abundance, but also from our need.

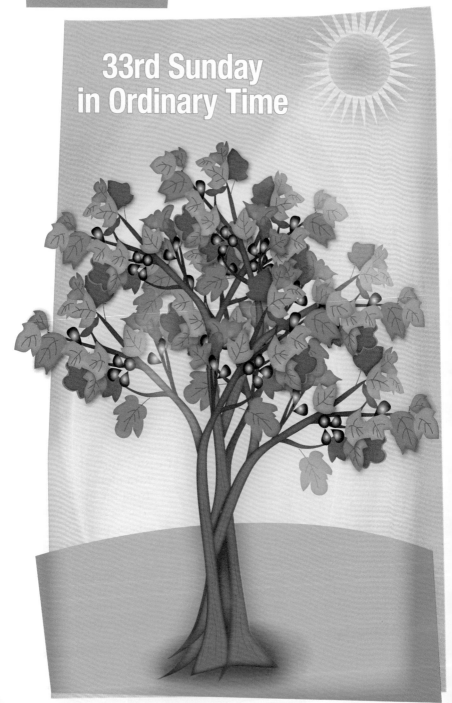

November 18

33rd Sunday in Ordinary Time

A reading from the book of the Prophet Daniel (12.1-3)

At that time Michael, the great prince, the protector of your people, shall arise. There shall be a time of anguish, such as has never occurred since nations first came into existence. But at that time your people shall be delivered, everyone who is found written in the book. Many of those who sleep in the dust of the earth shall awake, some to everlasting life, and some to shame and everlasting contempt.

Those who are wise shall shine like the brightness of the sky, and those who lead many to righteousness, like the stars forever and ever.

The word of the Lord. **Thanks be to God.**

Psalm 16

R̶ **Protect me, O God, for in you I take refuge.**

The Lord is my chosen portion and my cup;
you hold my lot.
I keep the Lord always before me;
because he is at my right hand, I shall not be moved. R̶

Therefore my heart is glad, and my soul rejoices;
my body also rests secure.
For you do not give me up to Sheol,
or let your faithful one see the Pit. R̶

You show me the path of life.
In your presence there is fullness of joy;
in your right hand are pleasures
forevermore. R̶

A reading from the Letter to the Hebrews (10.11-14, 18)

Every priest stands day after day at his service, offering again and again the same sacrifices that can never take away sins.

But when Christ had offered for all time a single sacrifice for sins, "he sat down at the right hand of God," and since then has been waiting "until his enemies would be made a footstool for his feet." For by a single offering he has perfected for all time those who are sanctified.

Where there is forgiveness of sin and lawless deeds, there is no longer any offering for sin.

The word of the Lord. **Thanks be to God.**

A reading from the holy Gospel according to Mark (13.24-32)

Jesus spoke to his disciples about the end which is to come:

"In those days, after the time of suffering, the sun will be darkened, and the moon will not give its light, and the stars will be falling from heaven, and the powers in the heavens will be shaken.

"Then they will see 'the Son of Man coming in clouds' with great power and glory. Then he will send out the Angels, and gather his elect from the four winds, from the ends of the earth to the ends of heaven.

"From the fig tree learn its lesson: as soon as its branch becomes tender and puts forth its leaves, you know that summer is near. So also, when you see these things taking place, you know that he is near, at the very gates.

"Truly I tell you, this generation will not pass away until all these things have taken place. Heaven and earth will pass away, but my words will not pass away.

"But about that day or hour no one knows, neither the Angels in heaven, nor the Son, but only the Father."

The Gospel of the Lord. **Praise to you, Lord Jesus Christ.**

The book of Daniel gave the Hebrew people comfort and hope in hard times. It was written about 160 years before Jesus was born, and is the first book of the Bible to talk about the resurrection of the dead.

Michael is the name of the angel who is the head of the heavenly angels and the protector of the people of Israel. His name means "who is like God" and is thought to show that no one is like God — God is all-good and all-powerful. At the end of time, Michael will lead an army and help the people overcome all suffering.

To be sanctified is to be made holy, as God is holy. We say people who are close to God are sanctified because they love everyone the way God does. The Letter to the Hebrews tells us that because Jesus has offered his life as a sacrifice for us, we are made holy for all time.

Although no one knows the day or hour when the world will end, we trust in God. We do not need to listen to people who claim that the world will end on a certain day. If we live as God's people and follow the life and teachings of Jesus, we will be ready whenever it happens.

Christ the King

A reading from the book of the Prophet Daniel (7.13-14)

I had a dream and visions as I lay in bed. As I watched in the night visions, I saw one like a son of man coming with the clouds of heaven. And he came to the One who is Ancient of Days and was presented before him.

To him was given dominion and glory and kingship, that all peoples, nations and languages should serve him. His dominion is an everlasting dominion that shall not pass away, and his kingship is one that shall never be destroyed.

The word of the Lord. **Thanks be to God.**

Psalm 93

R. **The Lord is king; he is robed in majesty.**

The Lord is king, he is robed in majesty;
the Lord is robed,
he is girded with strength. R.

He has established the world; it shall never be moved;
your throne is established from of old;
you are from everlasting. R.

Your decrees are very sure;
holiness befits your house,
O Lord, forevermore. R.

A reading from the book of Revelation (1.5-8)

Jesus Christ is the faithful witness, the firstborn of the dead, and the ruler of the kings of the earth. To him who loves us and freed us from our sins by his blood, and made us to be a kingdom, priests serving his God and Father, to him be glory and dominion forever and ever. Amen.

Look! He is coming with the clouds; every eye will see him, even those who pierced him; and on his account all the tribes of the earth will lament. So it is to be. Amen.

"I am the Alpha and the Omega," says the Lord God, who is and who was and who is to come, the Almighty.

The word of the Lord. **Thanks be to God.**

A reading from the holy Gospel according to John (18.33-37)

Pilate asked Jesus, "Are you the King of the Jews?"

Jesus answered, "Do you ask this on your own, or did others tell you about me?"

Pilate replied, "I am not a Jew, am I? Your own nation and the chief priests have handed you over to me. What have you done?"

Jesus answered, "My kingdom is not from this world. If my kingdom were from this world, my followers would be fighting to keep me from being handed over to the Jews. But as it is, my kingdom is not from here."

Pilate asked him, "So you are a king?"

Jesus answered, "You say that I am a king. For this I was born, and for this I came into the world, to testify to the truth. Everyone who belongs to the truth listens to my voice."

The Gospel of the Lord. **Praise to you, Lord Jesus Christ.**

The liturgical year, or church year, has five seasons: Advent, Christmas, Lent, Easter and Ordinary Time. See page 32 of this book to learn more. With the feast of Christ the King, we come to the end of Ordinary Time and of the liturgical year. Next Sunday we begin a new liturgical year with Advent.

Daniel calls God the One who is Ancient of Days as a way to show how God is eternal — his kingdom will have no end.

Dominion is a word meaning the authority to govern. To the Hebrew people, God's dominion extended to all peoples, all creation, heaven and hell. God is ruler over all.

The book of Revelation, also called the Apocalypse, is the last book in the Bible. It uses symbols and colourful images to tell its story. It was written at a time when the Church was being persecuted, and gives a vision of the end of time.

Alpha and Omega (A and Ω) are the first and last letters of the Greek alphabet. This expression describing Jesus means he is 'the beginning and the end' or the most important person in all of history.

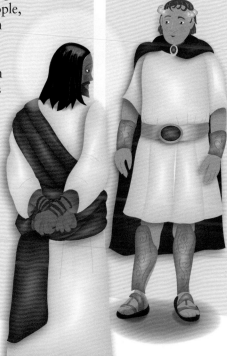

The days are surely coming, says the Lord, when I will fulfill the promise I made to the house of Israel and the house of Judah.

In those days and at that time I will cause a righteous Branch to spring up for David; and he shall execute justice and righteousness in the land.

In those days Judah will be saved and Jerusalem will live in safety. And this is the name by which it will be called: "The Lord is our righteousness."

The word of the Lord. **Thanks be to God.**

Psalm 25

R. **To you, O Lord, I lift my soul.**

Make me to know your ways, O Lord,
teach me your paths.
Lead me in your truth and teach me,
for you are the God of my salvation. R.

Good and upright is the Lord;
therefore he instructs sinners in the way.
He leads the humble in what is right,
and teaches the humble his way. R.

All the paths of the Lord are steadfast love and faithfulness,
for those who keep his covenant and his decrees.
The friendship of the Lord is for those who fear him,
and he makes his covenant known to them. R.

Brothers and sisters: May the Lord make you increase and abound in love for one another and for all, just as we abound in love for you. And may he so strengthen your hearts in holiness that you may be blameless before our God and Father at the coming of our Lord Jesus with all his saints.

Finally, brothers and sisters, we ask and urge you in the Lord Jesus that, as you learned from us how you ought to live and to please God, as, in fact, you are doing, you should do so more and more. For you know what instructions we gave you through the Lord Jesus.

The word of the Lord. **Thanks be to God.**

Jesus spoke to his disciples: "There will be signs in the sun, the moon, and the stars and on the earth distress among nations confused by the roaring of the sea and the waves. People will faint from fear and foreboding of what is coming upon the world, for the powers of the heavens will be shaken.

"Then they will see 'the Son of Man coming in a cloud' with power and great glory. Now when these things begin to take place, stand up and raise your heads, because your redemption is drawing near.

"Be on guard so that your hearts are not weighed down with dissipation and drunkenness and the worries of this life, and that day catch you unexpectedly, like a trap. For it will come upon all who live on the face of the whole earth. Be alert at all times, praying that you may have the strength to escape all these things that will take place, and to stand before the Son of Man."

The Gospel of the Lord. **Praise to you, Lord Jesus Christ.**

With the season of Advent, which means 'coming,' we begin a new liturgical year. Advent lasts four weeks and during this time the liturgical colour is purple. Purple is the colour of waiting; it reminds us to prepare our hearts to celebrate the birth of Jesus at Christmas and his return at the end of time.

Jeremiah lived about 600 years before Jesus. When he was still very young, God called him to guide the people of Israel back to God. Many people ignored Jeremiah at first and sent him away. But when the people of Israel feared that God had stopped loving them, Jeremiah gave them hope that God would not abandon them.

At the time of Jeremiah, God's people were divided into two kingdoms: the house of Israel in the north and the house of Judah in the south. Jeremiah announces God's wish for both kingdoms to be united into one nation, under one covenant.

A Branch for David refers to the descendants of David: his children and all who would be born from them. When Jeremiah announces that God will raise up a new branch, he is speaking of the birth of Jesus, who will be born of the House of David.

Saint Paul wrote two letters to the Thessalonians, Christians who lived in the Greek city of Thessalonica. It was an important city in the Roman Empire. In this letter, Saint Paul praises the early Christians, explains the good news of Jesus to them, and encourages them to continue to love one another.

287

December 9

2nd Sunday of Advent

Take off the garment of your sorrow and affliction, O Jerusalem,
and put on forever the beauty of the glory from God.
Put on the robe of the righteousness that comes from God;
put on your head the diadem of the glory of the Everlasting;
for God will show your splendour everywhere under heaven.
For God will give you evermore the name,
"Righteous Peace, Godly Glory."

Arise, O Jerusalem, stand upon the height;
look toward the east,
and see your children gathered from west and east
at the word of the Holy One,
rejoicing that God has remembered them.
For they went out from you on foot,
led away by their enemies;
but God will bring them back to you,
carried in glory, as on a royal throne.

For God has ordered that every high mountain
and the everlasting hills be made low
and the valleys filled up, to make level ground,
so that Israel may walk safely in the glory of God.
The woods and every fragrant tree
have shaded Israel at God's command.
For God will lead Israel with joy,
in the light of his glory,
with the mercy and righteousness that come from him.

The word of the Lord. **Thanks be to God.**

R. **The Lord has done great things for us; we are filled with joy.**

When the Lord restored the fortunes of Zion,
we were like those who dream.
Then our mouth was filled with laughter,
and our tongue with shouts of joy. R.

Then it was said among the nations,
"The Lord has done great things for them."
The Lord has done great things for us,
and we rejoiced. R.

Restore our fortunes, O Lord,
like the watercourses in the desert of the Negev.
May those who sow in tears
reap with shouts of joy. R.

Those who go out weeping,
bearing the seed for sowing,
shall come home with shouts of joy,
carrying their sheaves. R.

A reading from the Letter of Saint Paul to the Philippians (1.3-6, 8-11)

Brothers and sisters, I thank my God every time I remember you, constantly praying with joy in every one of my prayers for all of you, because of your sharing in the Gospel from the first day until now.

I am confident of this, that the one who began a good work among you will bring it to completion by the day of Jesus Christ.

For God is my witness, how I long for all of you with the compassion of Christ Jesus. And this is my prayer, that your love may overflow more and more with knowledge and full insight to help you determine what is best, so that in the day of Christ you may be pure and blameless, having produced the harvest of righteousness that comes through Jesus Christ for the glory and praise of God.

The word of the Lord. **Thanks be to God.**

In the fifteenth year of the reign of Emperor Tiberius, when Pontius Pilate was governor of Judea, and Herod was ruler of Galilee, and his brother Philip ruler of the region of Ituraea and Trachonitis, and Lysanias ruler of Abilene, during the high priesthood of Annas and Caiaphas, the word of God came to John son of Zechariah in the wilderness.

He went into all the region around the Jordan, proclaiming a baptism of repentance for the forgiveness of sins, as it is written in the book of the words of the Prophet Isaiah, "The voice of one crying out in the wilderness: 'Prepare the way of the Lord, make his paths straight. Every valley shall be filled, and every mountain and hill shall be made low, and the crooked shall be made straight, and the rough ways made smooth; and all flesh shall see the salvation of God.'"

The Gospel of the Lord.
Praise to you,
Lord Jesus Christ.

The book of the Prophet Baruch was written about 200 years before Jesus was born. It tells the story of the people of Israel while they were forced to live in Babylon. Baruch urges them to follow God and trust in him.

To gather from west and east means to come from all across the world. The Prophet Baruch sees a time when all people will come together and live in peace.

Saint Paul wrote to the Philippians, a community of Christians in the Greek city of Philippi. This was one of the earliest Christian communities founded by Saint Paul and he felt great affection for it. He thanks them for their help and encourages them to keep their faith in Jesus strong.

Emperor Tiberius was the successor to Emperor Augustus who had been emperor at the time of the birth of Jesus. Tiberius ruled the Roman Empire during most of Jesus' lifetime.

At the time of Jesus' birth, the province of Judea was under Roman rule and Pontius Pilate was the Roman governor. The Jewish people were longing for a leader who could free them from their Roman oppressors, just as Moses had led the people from slavery in Egypt.

Herod was the Jewish ruler of Galilee, a small area of the Roman Empire, during the time of the Emperor Tiberius. This Herod was a son of King Herod who ruled at the time of Jesus' birth.

A baptism of repentance is a sign that a person wants to turn back to God. John the Baptist baptized people in the River Jordan to show that their sins were washed away. Today, the sacrament of baptism unites us with Jesus and makes us part of the Church.

Sing aloud, O daughter Zion; shout, O Israel!
Rejoice and exult with all your heart,
O daughter of Jerusalem!
The Lord has taken away the judgments against you,
he has turned away your enemies.
The king of Israel, the Lord, is in your midst;
you shall fear disaster no more.

On that day it shall be said to Jerusalem:
Do not fear, O Zion;
do not let your hands grow weak.
The Lord, your God, is in your midst,
a warrior who gives victory;
he will rejoice over you with gladness,
he will renew you in his love.
The Lord, your God, will exult over you with loud singing
as on a day of festival.

The word of the Lord. **Thanks be to God.**

R. **Shout aloud and sing for joy:**
great in your midst is the Holy One of Israel.

Surely God is my salvation;
I will trust, and will not be afraid,
for the Lord God is my strength and my might;
he has become my salvation.
With joy you will draw water
from the wells of salvation. R.

Give thanks to the Lord,
call on his name;
make known his deeds among the nations;
proclaim that his name is exalted. R.

Sing praises to the Lord,
for he has done gloriously;
let this be known in all the earth.
Shout aloud and sing for joy, O royal Zion,
for great in your midst
is the Holy One of Israel. R.

A reading from the Letter of Saint Paul to the Philippians (4.4-7)

Rejoice in the Lord always; again I will say, Rejoice.

Let your gentleness be known to everyone. The Lord is near. Do not worry about anything, but in everything by prayer and supplication with thanksgiving let your requests be made known to God.

And the peace of God, which surpasses all understanding, will guard your hearts and your minds in Christ Jesus.

The word of the Lord. **Thanks be to God.**

The crowds, who were gathering to be baptized by John, asked him, "What should we do?" In reply John said to them, "Whoever has two coats must share with anyone who has none; and whoever has food must do likewise."

Even tax collectors came to be baptized, and they asked him, "Teacher, what should we do?" He said to them, "Collect no more than the amount prescribed for you." Soldiers also asked him, "And we, what should we do?" He said to them, "Do not extort money from anyone by threats or false accusation, and be satisfied with your wages."

As the people were filled with expectation, and all were questioning in their hearts concerning John, whether he might be the Messiah, John answered all of them by saying, "I baptize you with water; but one who is more powerful than I is coming; I am not worthy to untie the thong of his sandals. He will baptize you with the Holy Spirit and fire. His winnowing fork is in his hand, to clear his threshing floor and to gather the wheat into his granary; but the chaff he will burn with unquenchable fire."

So, with many other exhortations, John proclaimed the good news to the people.

The Gospel of the Lord.
Praise to you, Lord Jesus Christ.

The Prophet Zephaniah lived about 700 years before Jesus was born. The people of Israel had fallen away from their faith. Zephaniah tried to help them return to God.

Zion was the name of a hill in Jerusalem, where the temple was built Often the city itself and the whole people of Israel were called Zion. Daughter Zion is another way of naming the entire nation, the whole people of God.

Saint Paul tells the Philippians to rejoice always because we all live in the Lord. Nothing can separate us from God's love. In Latin 'rejoice' is *gaudete*: the Third Sunday of Advent is also known as Gaudete Sunday because of Saint Paul's call to rejoice. On Advent wreaths, the pink candle is lit today.

The Jewish people didn't like tax collectors because they worked for the Romans, who were enemies of Israel. Also, many tax collectors cheated people and took more money than they needed for taxes.

To extort money is to force people to give money against their will. John the Baptist tells tax collectors that while they have an unpopular job to do, it is important that they do it fairly without cheating people.

A winnowing fork is a big wooden tool for separating the grain, which is good to eat, from its husk, which is not edible. It separates the good from the bad. John the Baptist uses it as a symbol Jesus' power.

4th Sunday of Advent

The Lord says to his people:
"You, O Bethlehem of Ephrathah,
who are one of the little clans of Judea,
from you shall come forth for me
one who is to rule in Israel,
whose origin is from of old, from ancient days."

Therefore he shall give them up until the time
when she who is in labour has brought forth;
then the rest of his kindred
shall return to the children of Israel.
And he shall stand and feed his flock
in the strength of the Lord,
in the majesty of the name of the Lord his God.

And they shall live secure,
for now he shall be great to the ends of the earth;
and he shall be peace.

The word of the Lord. **Thanks be to God.**

Psalm 80

R. **Restore us, O God; let your face shine, that we may be saved.**

Give ear, O Shepherd of Israel,
you who are enthroned upon the cherubim, shine forth.
Stir up your might,
and come to save us. R.

Turn again, O God of hosts;
look down from heaven, and see;
have regard for this vine,
the stock that your right hand has planted. R.

But let your hand be upon the man at your right,
the son of man you have made strong for yourself.
Then we will never turn back from you;
give us life, and we will call on your name. R.

A reading from the Letter to the Hebrews (10.5-10)

Brothers and sisters: When Christ came into the world, he said, "Sacrifices and offerings you have not desired, but a body you have prepared for me; in burnt offerings and sin offerings you have taken no pleasure. Then I said, as it is written of me in the scroll of the book, 'See, God, I have come to do your will, O God.'"

When Christ said, "You have neither desired nor taken pleasure in sacrifices and offerings and burnt offerings and sin offerings" (these are offered according to the Law), then he added, "See, I have come to do your will." He abolishes the first in order to establish the second.

And it is by God's will that we have been sanctified through the offering of the body of Jesus Christ once for all.

The word of the Lord. **Thanks be to God.**

A reading from the holy Gospel according to Luke (1.39-45)

Mary set out and went with haste to a Judean town in the hill country, where she entered the house of Zechariah and greeted Elizabeth.

When Elizabeth heard Mary's greeting, the child leaped in her womb. And Elizabeth was filled with the Holy Spirit and exclaimed with a loud cry, "Blessed are you among women, and blessed is the fruit of your womb. And why has this happened to me, that the mother of my Lord comes to me? For as soon as I heard the sound of your greeting, the child in my womb leaped for joy. And blessed is she who believed that there would be a fulfillment of what was spoken to her by the Lord."

The Gospel of the Lord. **Praise to you, Lord Jesus Christ.**

Micah was a prophet who lived about 700 years before Jesus was born. It was a hard time for Israel. The Assyrians were taking over and the Israelites were not working together or helping the poor. Micah told them God was angry at them, but there was hope: if they changed their ways, things would get better.

Bethlehem ('house of bread' in Hebrew) is the traditional birthplace of King David, one of Jesus' ancestors. It is a city located south of Jerusalem, and is Jesus' birthplace also. See the map on page 320.

God asked Mary, a young woman who was engaged to marry Joseph, to be the mother of his son, Jesus. She said yes. We are thankful for Mary's generosity because, through her son Jesus, we have eternal life. Since Jesus is our brother, Mary his mother is also our mother. She listens to our prayers and presents them to Jesus for us.

Elizabeth, Mary's cousin, became pregnant at an age when women can no longer have children. Her husband, Zechariah, was a priest of the temple in Jerusalem. Their son, John the Baptist, Jesus' cousin, was six months older than Jesus.

"Blessed are you among women." With these words of praise, Elizabeth tells Mary that she is indeed special to God. Mary is the best model for Christians of all ages and is called the First Disciple. We repeat Elizabeth's words each time we pray the Hail Mary.

Christmas
The Nativity of the Lord

A reading from the book of the Prophet Isaiah
(9.2-4, 6-7)

The people who walked in darkness have seen a great light;
those who lived in a land of deep darkness —
on them light has shone.
You have multiplied the nation,
you have increased its joy;
they rejoice before you
as with joy at the harvest,
as people exult when dividing plunder.

For the yoke of their burden,
and the bar across their shoulders,
the rod of their oppressor,
you have broken as on the day of Midian.

For a child has been born for us,
a son given to us;
authority rests upon his shoulders;
and he is named
Wonderful Counsellor, Mighty God,
Everlasting Father, Prince of Peace.

His authority shall grow continually,
and there shall be endless peace
for the throne of David and his kingdom.
He will establish and uphold it
with justice and with righteousness
from this time onward and forevermore.
The zeal of the Lord of hosts will do this.

The word of the Lord. **Thanks be to God.**

R. **Today is born our Saviour, Christ the Lord.**

O sing to the Lord a new song;
sing to the Lord, all the earth.
Sing to the Lord, bless his name;
tell of his salvation from day to day. R.

Declare his glory among the nations,
his marvellous works among all the peoples.
For great is the Lord, and greatly to be praised;
he is to be revered above all gods. R.

Let the heavens be glad, and let the earth rejoice;
let the sea roar, and all that fills it;
let the field exult, and everything in it.
Then shall all the trees of the forest sing for joy. R.

Rejoice before the Lord; for he is coming,
for he is coming to judge the earth.
He will judge the world with righteousness,
and the peoples with his truth. R.

A reading from the Letter of Saint Paul to Titus
(2.11-14)

Beloved: The grace of God has appeared, bringing salvation to all, training us to renounce impiety and worldly passions, and in the present age to live lives that are self-controlled, upright, and godly, while we wait for the blessed hope and the manifestation of the glory of our great God and Saviour, Jesus Christ.

He it is who gave himself for us that he might redeem us from all iniquity and purify for himself a people of his own who are zealous for good deeds.

The word of the Lord. **Thanks be to God.**

In those days a decree went out from Caesar Augustus that all the world should be registered. This was the first registration and was taken while Quirinius was governor of Syria. All went to their own towns to be registered. Joseph also went from the town of Nazareth in Galilee to Judea, to the city of David called Bethlehem, because he was descended from the house and family of David. He went to be registered with Mary, to whom he was engaged and who was expecting a child.

While they were there, the time came for her to deliver her child. And she gave birth to her firstborn son and wrapped him in swaddling clothes, and laid him in a manger, because there was no place for them in the inn.

In that region there were shepherds living in the fields, keeping watch over their flock by night. Then an Angel of the Lord stood before them, and the glory of the Lord shone around them, and they were terrified. But the Angel said to them, "Do not be afraid; for see — I am bringing you good news of great joy for all the people: to you is born this day in the city of David a Saviour, who is the Christ, the Lord. This will be a sign for you: you will find a child wrapped in swaddling clothes and lying in a manger."

And suddenly there was with the Angel a multitude of the heavenly host, praising God and saying, "Glory to God in the highest heaven, and on earth peace among those whom he favours!"

When the Angels had left them and gone into heaven, the shepherds said to one another, "Let us go now to Bethlehem and see this thing that has taken place, which the Lord has made known to us." So they went with haste and found Mary and Joseph, and the child lying in the manger.

The Gospel of the Lord.
Praise to you, Lord Jesus Christ.

Christmas Day is celebrated on December 25th, but the Christmas season lasts up to three weeks, ending with the Baptism of Jesus in January. The liturgical colour for this season is white, the colour of joy and celebration.

Prophets like Isaiah were good men and women who spoke for God. Sometimes their messages were demanding: they asked people to change their lives and attitudes in order to grow closer to God. At other times, they brought words of comfort.

The coming of our Saviour is such a great event that even the heavens, earth, sea and trees sing for joy! Our hearts are full of happiness: God has come to be with his people.

A manger is a wooden crate filled with hay to feed the animals in a stable. The baby Jesus was placed in a manger soon after he was born. It was amazing that God would choose to be born in such a simple place.

In the Bible, an Angel of the Lord is a messenger of God. Angels appear many times in the story of the birth of Jesus: announcing Jesus' birth to Mary; appearing three times to Joseph in dreams; and appearing in the heavens on Christmas night.

Glory to God in the highest and on earth peace to all people!

Merry Christmas!

Holy Family of Jesus, Mary and Joseph

In due time Hannah conceived and bore a son. She named him Samuel, for she said, "I have asked him of the Lord." Elkanah and all his household went up to offer to the Lord the yearly sacrifice, and to pay his vow. But Hannah did not go up, for she said to her husband, "As soon as the child is weaned, I will bring him, that he may appear in the presence of the Lord, and remain there forever; I will offer him as a nazirite for all time."

When she had weaned him, she took him up with her, along with a three-year-old bull, a measure of flour, and a skin of wine. She brought him to the house of the Lord at Shiloh; and the child was young. Then they slaughtered the bull, and they brought the child to Eli. And she said, "Oh, my lord! As you live, my lord, I am the woman who was standing here in your presence, praying to the Lord. For this child I prayed; and the Lord has granted me the petition that I made to him. Therefore I have lent him to the Lord; as long as he lives, he is given to the Lord." She left him there for the Lord.

The word of the Lord. **Thanks be to God.**

Psalm 84

℟ **Blessed are those who live in your house, O Lord.**

How lovely is your dwelling place,
O Lord of hosts!
My soul longs, indeed it faints for the courts of the Lord;
my heart and my flesh sing for joy to the living God. ℟

Blessed are those who live in your house,
ever singing your praise.
Blessed are those whose strength is in you,
in whose heart are the highways to Zion. ℟

O Lord God of hosts, hear my prayer;
give ear, O God of Jacob!
Behold our shield, O God;
look on the face of your anointed. ℟

For a day in your courts is better
than a thousand elsewhere.
I would rather be a doorkeeper in the house of my God
than live in the tents of wickedness. ℟

Beloved: See what love the Father has given us, that we should be called children of God; and that is what we are. The reason the world does not know us is that it did not know him. Beloved, we are God's children now; what we will be has not yet been revealed. What we do know is this: when he is revealed, we will be like him, for we will see him as he is.

Beloved, if our hearts do not condemn us, we have boldness before God; and we receive from him whatever we ask, because we obey his commandments and do what pleases him. And this is his commandment, that we should believe in the name of his Son Jesus Christ and love one another, just as he has commanded us. Whoever obeys his commandments abides in him, and he abides in them. And by this we know that he abides in us, by the Spirit that he has given us.

The word of the Lord. **Thanks be to God.**

Every year the parents of Jesus went to Jerusalem for the festival of the Passover. And when he was twelve years old, they went up as usual for the festival.

When the festival was ended and they started to return, the boy Jesus stayed behind in Jerusalem, but his parents did not know it. Assuming that he was in the group of travellers, they went a day's journey. Then they started to look for him among their relatives and friends. When they did not find him, they returned to Jerusalem to search for him.

After three days they found him in the temple, sitting among the teachers, listening to them and asking them questions. And all who heard him were amazed at his understanding and his answers. When his parents saw him they were astonished; and his mother said to him, "Child, why have you treated us like this? Look, your father and I have been searching for you in great anxiety." He said to them, "Why were you searching for me? Did you not know that I must be in my Father's house?" But they did not understand what he said to them.

Then he went down with them and came to Nazareth, and was obedient to them. His mother treasured all these things in her heart. And Jesus increased in wisdom and in years, and in favour with God and human beings.

The Gospel of the Lord. **Praise to you, Lord Jesus Christ.**

The Holy Family is Mary, Joseph and Jesus. Because they are a real family, they understand and are close to every family. Our own family is a gift from God. We take care of this gift when we share our lives, listen to one another and pray together.

Samuel, a prophet and judge in Israel, was born over 1,000 years before Jesus. The Lord chose Samuel to anoint Saul, the first king of Israel. He also anointed David, who was king after Saul and Jesus' ancestor. The Bible contains two books in his name: 1 Samuel and 2 Samuel.

A nazirite ('consecrated' or 'set apart') was a person who had taken a vow to live a life dedicated to God. In her gratitude to God, Hannah makes this vow for her son Samuel on his behalf.

Eli was the chief priest at the sanctuary at Shiloh, which was the centre of worship. His task was to guard the sanctuary, especially the Ark of the Covenant that was kept there.

In his letter, Saint John uses the term the world to refer to people who think only about things like money and having fun. Worldly people often find it difficult to make room in their hearts for Jesus.

The teachers in the temple were men who spent their lives studying the Bible and sharing their knowledge with the people. They were very wise and would not have expected a child to speak as well as the young Jesus did.

Morning Prayers

A Child's Prayer for Morning

Now, before I run to play,
let me not forget to pray
to God who kept me through the night
and waked me with the morning light.
Help me, Lord, to love you more
than I have ever loved before.
In my work and in my play
please be with me through the day.
Amen.

Morning Prayer

Dear God, we thank you for this day.
We thank you for our families and friends.
We thank you for our classmates.
Be with us as we work and play today.
Help us always to be kind to each other.
We pray in the name of the Father,
and of the Son and of the Holy Spirit. Amen.

(Heather Reid, *Let's Pray! Prayers for the Elementary Classroom*. Ottawa;
Novalis: 2006)

Angel of God

Angel of God, my guardian dear,
to whom God's love entrusts me here,
ever this day be at my side,
to light and guard, to rule and guide. Amen.

Evening Prayers

Children's Bedtime Prayer

Now I lay me down to sleep,
I pray you, Lord, your child to keep.
Your love will guard me through the night
and wake me with the morning light. Amen.

Child's Evening Prayer

I hear no voice, I feel no touch,
I see no glory bright;
but yet I know that God is near,
in darkness as in light.
He watches ever by my side,
and hears my whispered prayer:
the Father for his little child
both night and day does care.

God Hear My Prayer

God in heaven hear my prayer,
keep me in your loving care.
Be my guide in all I do,
bless all those who love me too. Amen.

Mealtime Prayers

Grace before Meals

Bless us, O Lord,
and these your gifts
which we are about to receive
from your bounty.
Through Christ our Lord. Amen.

❋ ❋ ❋

For food in a world where many walk in hunger,
for friends in a world where many walk alone,
for faith in a world where many walk in fear,
we give you thanks, O God. Amen.

❋ ❋ ❋

God is great, God is good!
Let us thank God for our food. Amen.

❋ ❋ ❋

Be present at our table, Lord.
Be here and everywhere adored.
Your creatures bless
and grant that we may feast
in paradise with you. Amen.

Grace after Meals

We give you thanks, Almighty God,
for these and all the benefits
we receive from your bounty.
Through Christ our Lord. Amen.

❋ ❋ ❋

Traditional Prayers

Lord's Prayer

Our Father, who art in heaven,
hallowed be thy name;
thy kingdom come,
thy will be done on earth as it is in heaven.
Give us this day our daily bread,
and forgive us our trespasses,
as we forgive those who trespass against us;
and lead us not into temptation,
but deliver us from evil. Amen.

Hail Mary

Hail Mary, full of grace,
the Lord is with you.
Blessed are you among women and
blessed is the fruit of your womb, Jesus.
Holy Mary, Mother of God,
pray for us sinners,
now and at the hour of our death. Amen.

Glory Be to the Father

Glory be to the Father,
and to the Son,
and to the Holy Spirit.
As it was in the beginning,
is now, and ever shall be,
world without end. Amen.

More Prayers

Prayer for Friends

Loving God, you are the best friend we can have.

We ask today that you help us to be good friends
    to each other.

Help us to be fair, kind and unselfish.

Keep our friends safe and happy.

Bless us and bless all friends in this community.

We pray in the name of Jesus,

who was always the friend of children. Amen.

(Heather Reid, *Let's Pray! Prayers for the Elementary Classroom.*
Ottawa; Novalis: 2006)

In the Silence

If we really want to pray,
we must first learn to listen,
for in the silence of the heart,
God speaks.
(Blessed Teresa of Calcutta, 1910-1997)

Family Prayer

Father, what love you have given us.
May we love as you would have us love.
Teach us to be kind to each other,
patient and gentle with one another.
Help us to bear all things together,
to see in our love, your love,
through Christ our Lord. Amen.

Prayer for the Birthday Child

May God bless you with every good gift
and surround you with love and happiness.
May Jesus be your friend and guide
all the days of your life.
May the Spirit of God guide your footsteps
in the path of truth. Amen.

Prayer for Pets

Dear Father, hear and bless
your beasts and singing birds,
and guard with care and tenderness
small things that have no words. Amen.

When Someone Has Died

Lord God, hear our cries.
Grant us comfort in our sadness,
gently wipe away our tears,
and give us courage in the days ahead.
We ask this through Christ our Lord. Amen.

Palestine 2,000 years ago

When Jesus lived here...

- Palestine was a small country, occupied by soldiers of the Roman Empire. Jerusalem was the capital city.
- The country already had a very long history. It was in a part of the world we call the "cradle of civilization."
- Travellers from all around the Mediterranean Sea and the Far East passed through Palestine. Neighbours and visitors included Egyptians, Phoenicians, Syrians, Parthians, Nabateans, Greeks and many others.
- Many citizens understood several languages, including Aramaic, Hebrew, Greek and Latin.

Three horizontal divisions:

- North: Galilee (area #2 on the map) is an area of pleasant weather. Jesus spent most of his life here.
- Central: Samaria (area #3) reaches from the sea coast to the mountain range.
- South: Judea (area #1) is a mountainous region with harsh, dry weather.

Four geographic regions (vertical strips):

- The coastal plain: a broad, flat section along the coast, wide in the south and narrower in the north. Summers here are hot and humid.
- The mountain chain: dry and desert in the south; more fertile valleys in the north.
- The deep ravine: the Jordan Rift Valley splits the mountain range in two, with the Sea of Galilee at one end of the rift and the Jordan River flowing south to the Dead Sea at the other end.
- The plateau: a high, flat area beyond the mountains on the east side of the Jordan River.

Palestine today:

Most of the country where Jesus lived is now called 'Israel.' It is bordered by Lebanon to the north, Syria and Jordan to the east, and Egypt to the south.

1. Judea
2. Galilee
3. Samaria
4. Phoenicia
5. Perea
6. Decapolis
7. Syria and Tetrarchy of Philip
8. Idumea

EGYPT

ORDER YOUR 2013 SUNDAY MISSAL FOR YOUNG CATHOLICS TODAY!

2013 SUNDAY MISSAL FOR YOUNG CATHOLICS

ONLY $9.95!

Call for quantity prices.

QTY	ITEM NO.	TITLE	UNIT PRICE	TOTAL
	171059	2013 Sunday Missal for Young Catholics*	$9.95	
			Shipping	
			TOTAL DUE	

SHIPPING AND HANDLING

$1.00 to $60.00.............$6.00
$61.00 to $99.00 ....$7.00
$100.00 and up ....FREE

*All taxes are included in the per copy price. **All orders must be prepaid.** Price is subject to change without notice.

Name

Address

City   Prov   Postal Code

E-mail   ( )
                                                    Phone Number

❑ Payment enclosed (please do not send cash)

Charge my ❑ VISA **VISA**   ❑ Mastercard *MasterCard*

Card No.   Expiry Date   /   Signature

Name on Card   YM13

TO ORDER Call: 1-800-387-7164 • Fax: 1-877-702-7775 • E-mail: resources@novalis.ca
Mail to: Novalis, 10 Lower Spadina Ave., Ste. 400, Toronto, ON M5V 2Z2

Palestine 2,000 years ago

When Jesus lived here…

- Palestine was a small country, occupied by soldiers of the Roman Empire. Jerusalem was the capital city.
- The country already had a very long history. It was in a part of the world we call the "cradle of civilization."
- Travellers from all around the Mediterranean Sea and the Far East passed through Palestine. Neighbours and visitors included Egyptians, Phoenicians, Syrians, Parthians, Nabateans, Greeks and many others.
- Many citizens understood several languages, including Aramaic, Hebrew, Greek and Latin.

Three horizontal divisions:

- North: Galilee (area #2 on the map) is an area of pleasant weather. Jesus spent most of his life here.
- Central: Samaria (area #3) reaches from the sea coast to the mountain range.
- South: Judea (area #1) is a mountainous region with harsh, dry weather.

Four geographic regions (vertical strips):

- The coastal plain: a broad, flat section along the coast, wide in the south and narrower in the north. Summers here are hot and humid.
- The mountain chain: dry and desert in the south; more fertile valleys in the north.
- The deep ravine: the Jordan Rift Valley splits the mountain range in two, with the Sea of Galilee at one end of the rift and the Jordan River flowing south to the Dead Sea at the other end.
- The plateau: a high, flat area beyond the mountains on the east side of the Jordan River.

Palestine today:

Most of the country where Jesus lived is now called 'Israel.' It is bordered by Lebanon to the north, Syria and Jordan to the east, and Egypt to the south.

1. Judea
2. Galilee
3. Samaria
4. Phoenicia
5. Perea
6. Decapolis
7. Syria and Tetrarchy of Philip
8. Idumea

EGYPT